IMBALANCED

12-18-21

Dear Ken & Anne,

Thanks for everything you do for Channing!

All the best,

Sam

IMBALANCED

—A Memoir—

SHERI THOMAS

LUMINARE PRESS
WWW.LUMINAREPRESS.COM

Imbalanced: A Memoir
Copyright © 2021 by Sheri Thomas

All rights reserved. This book or any portion thereof may not be reproduced or used in any manner whatsoever without the express written permission of the publisher, except for the use of brief quotations in a book review.

Printed in the United States of America

Luminare Press
442 Charnelton St.
Eugene, OR 97401
www.luminarepress.com

LCCN: 2021920233
ISBN: 978-1-64388-829-3

To my mother Carol,
Your love and determination made all the difference.

And to everyone with a disability
or mental health condition,
You are not alone, and you are worthy.

Two-Pound Baby Wins Life Fight

IMBALANCED traces Sheri Thomas' remarkable journey from a front-page headline in 1962 to her current role as an advocate fighting to remove the stigmas surrounding physical disabilities and mental health.

Unflinching, poignant and humorous, here is her personal account of juggling lifelong challenges—including cerebral palsy, migraines and brain surgery—with a successful career before unexpectedly facing serious mental health crises in her fifties. Sheri Thomas spent decades promoting full accessibility as part of various disability commissions and committees in Maryland. For a free copy of the author's *Lessons Learned* mental health tips or to contact Sheri Thomas, email tsheri1221@gmail.com.

Cover Photo: The author, age 6, (in pink coat and plaster casts) poses for an Easter picture with her grandparents and her mother, brother, sister and aunt in 1968.

Contents

Introduction 1

PART ONE:
Roots 3

PART TWO:
Step By Step 17

PART THREE:
The Write Stuff 67

PART FOUR:
Knock Knock 109

PART FIVE:
My True Self 123

PART SIX:
On Top of Everything 141

PART SEVEN:
From Top to Bottom
and Back Up Again 159

PART EIGHT:
Lessons Learned 205

Acknowledgements 213

Introduction

I started writing this book as therapy in January 2020 as I recovered emotionally and physically from a suicide attempt six months earlier.

In March 2020, a stay-at-home order was enacted globally to minimize the spread of the COVID-19 virus, which was killing thousands daily in the U.S. and around the world. Schools, businesses and restaurants were closed, and millions lost their jobs and income.

Stuck in the house with plenty of time for reflection, I started to write about my childhood with cerebral palsy in the 1960s and '70s, decades before the Americans With Disabilities Act (ADA) was signed into law. While writing this book, I uncovered a recent study that said that adults with cerebral palsy are at an increased risk of experiencing a mental health disorder. I am one of those people.

Unfortunately, I do not have my childhood medical records. They were lost during the many moves we made. While emptying out our storage locker in May, my husband Douglas found an old manilla envelope that my mother had given me in 1989, just after my wedding. Inside was my original birth certificate, my baptismal certificate, and a kindergarten report card, along with a cover letter and a short story entitled, "Step by Step," which she had sent to *Redbook* in 1969. Her story was never published. As I continued writing, I interspersed her words with mine, painting a fuller picture of my early life.

The story of my birth on December 21, 1961, was described as a miracle not only by my family but also on the front page of the Jefferson City, *Missouri Post-Tribune*. The headline of its February 21, 1962 issue was: "Two-Pound Baby Wins Life Fight." That baby was me, and the story celebrated my release from the hospital after spending months in an incubator struggling to survive. My homecoming news shared the page with "John Glenn in Excellent Condition After Three Obits of Globe."

My story by reporter Mark Sullivan begins, "Sheri Lynn Thomas is two today—not two years old but two months. For most little girls there isn't anything very special about being two months old, unless they, like Sheri Lynn, weighed less than three pounds at birth." The story continues, "She was six weeks early and weighed only two-pounds-11 ounces. Before she started gaining any weight, she had lost five of the precious ounces. Today she weighs five and a half pounds and is doing well. According to Memorial Hospital records, she is the smallest baby born at the hospital to survive."

My life would hang in the balance once again on June 28, 2019, as I woke up in an ambulance on the way to a Baltimore hospital.

PART ONE:

Roots

CHAPTER 1

From The Lighthouse

My maternal grandmother Naomi Gray, born in 1912, was the daughter of a lighthouse keeper in southern Maryland.

She married a wiry-built German named Otto Cantz. They struggled to raise their four girls, Arline, Joyce, my mother Carol (born in 1937) and Roberta, on meager funds in South Jersey near Camden and Burlington. Since there was no money during the Depression to buy new clothes, older children passed "hand-me-downs" to their younger siblings.

To satisfy her sweet tooth, my mother regularly ate most of the one tube of toothpaste Naomi could afford every couple of weeks.

Naomi and Otto later divorced, and she married Ed Colgan. He was dashingly handsome. I used to tease him by telling him he looked just like John Forsythe from the popular 1970s series *Dynasty*.

They had a much-loved son, Eddie, my mother's only remaining sibling. Ed Sr. and Naomi settled in Mount Holly, New Jersey, an idealistic small town that could have been painted by

Norman Rockwell, where Ed worked for the water company until he retired.

I never met my maternal grandfather Otto who ran a small Esso gas station. I've only seen him in old black and white photos. There is one of Otto in front of his Esso station in the early 1950s. There are faded photos of Otto with my mother and older sister Kim taken in the summer of 1958 when my mother took her firstborn from Wisconsin back to see family in New Jersey. On a warm summer day, Otto, balding and wearing a sleeveless white tee shirt, smiles as Kim takes baby steps in the grass, our mother holding both her hands high over her head.

A year later, Otto committed suicide in his garage by running an exhaust hose into the front seat of his car. When I asked my mother years ago why he committed suicide, she said that he had been unhappy and struggling financially. We never broached the topic again.

Naomi's oldest, my Aunt Arline, married my Uncle Harold in the late 1940s at the tender age of 15. They had two boys, Harold and Terry.

My cousin Harold, who went to high school with Meryl Streep in Bernardsville, New Jersey, would marry and have two children. Their son Buster, several years younger than me, was the second in our family to be born with cerebral palsy.

There were scant resources in the early 1970s to care for severely disabled children at home. Buster, unlike me, was unable to control his limbs or speech and needed continuous care, so he lived at a school for children with disabilities in North Jersey.

Buster's parents would sometimes take him home for the weekend. On one occasion, when I was around 10, there was a big party for my Grandmother Naomi's birthday, and Buster was there. I didn't say hello to him, because I was ashamed that I could walk and talk. I have some old polaroid pictures from that party with everyone's face in them except Buster's. Only his legs and the bottom of his wheelchair are visible.

My Aunt Arline was followed a few years later by her younger sister, my Aunt Joyce. Joyce would marry young as most women did in the 1950s, to my darkly handsome Uncle Gene. They had three children, my cousins Gene, Terry and Joy. Throughout most of her adult life, Joyce struggled with manic depression, now referred to as bipolar.

She was often in and out of a psychiatric hospital in South Jersey called Ancora, where she would stay until her lithium levels evened out and she was stable enough to return home. Once home, she would often go off her medication and become unstable again and have to be readmitted to the hospital to start the treatment cycle all over again.

Over 50 years later, in 2014, I too would be diagnosed as bipolar.

CHAPTER 2

To The Prairie

My paternal grandfather William Thomas was born in 1914 in Marshfield, Wisconsin. He married Sylvia Feit, also born in 1914, in the early 1930s during the Depression, just as President Franklin Roosevelt was enacting the New Deal to put many unemployed Americans to work. His administration created the Rural Electrification Administration (REA) in 1935. At the time, large electric companies were refusing to build electric lines in sparsely populated areas because it was unprofitable, leaving 90 percent of the homes and farms in rural America in the dark.

William became an early pioneer in the country's rural electrification efforts, and he later headed the Wisconsin Electric Cooperative Association where farmers and other members could obtain low-interest government loans through the REA to build electric lines to rural Wisconsin. Today, more than 42 million customers are served by rural electrification systems, including over 600,000 in Wisconsin.

I have a treasured photo of my grandparents standing next to President Kennedy in the Rose Garden in front of a large group attending a *Cooperatives and the Future* conference in Washington, D.C. in April 1963. They were proud to have a young, vibrant President their age who also shared their Catholic faith and were devastated when he was assassinated a few months later. I didn't see the picture or know about the important work my grandfather did until well into adulthood.

My grandparents settled in Madison, Wisconsin and had four children: my dad Floyd (called Bill) in 1936, Paul (1940), Mary Ann (1946), and Jane a few years later.

Paul and Mary Ann were born with muscular dystrophy, a genetic disorder that causes progressive muscle degeneration and weakness. Paul died in 1952 at the age of 11, and Mary Ann died in 1965 at 19. My grandparents were ardent supporters of the Muscular Dystrophy Association, and Mary Ann and Paul had both served as poster children for its annual telethon.

As a child, I always watched the Muscular Dystrophy Association's Labor Day Telethons hosted by Jerry Lewis with both horror and wonder. I realized that many of the children I saw paraded across my black and white television screen in braces and wheelchairs would soon be dead. And I wondered why I had been born with cerebral palsy instead of the fatal disease that killed Paul and Mary Ann who smiled at me from a big framed black and white photograph at my grandparents' home in Madison, Wisconsin.

Newspaper photo of my paternal grandparents, William and Sylvia Thomas, with President John F. Kennedy in the Rose Garden in April 1963. My grandfather is standing next to the President (in the light-colored raincoat and glasses) and my grandmother is smiling, wearing a rain bonnet.

CHAPTER 3

In The Navy

My fun-loving mother, Carol, wore poodle skirts and danced on a show that was later renamed *American Bandstand*. To the dismay of my grandmother, she also rode on the back of her boyfriend's motorcycle.

When Mom graduated high school in 1955, she joined the Navy to "see the world." Instead, she was stationed at the Philadelphia Naval Yard, less than a half hour from her New Jersey home.

She went through boot camp at the Bainbridge U.S. Naval Training center in Port Deposit, Maryland, where she met my father, Bill Thomas, a tall, dark-haired charmer who had been recalled to active duty after serving as a part-time reservist in Wisconsin.

It was a time when "good girls" waited to have sex until they were married. Just a few months after that first meeting, Carol and Bill were engaged. My mother felt she had waited long enough. They planned a New Jersey wedding for the summer of 1956.

Dad's mother Sylvia called Mom to say that she and her husband William would be flying from

Wisconsin to New Jersey with their daughters, 5-year-old Janey (as my aunt was called as a child) who would be the flower girl, and 10-year-old Mary Ann, who wore leg braces and used a wheelchair.

After she hung up, Mom asked Dad why his sister Mary Ann needed a wheelchair. "Oh, she has muscular dystrophy. My brother Paul had it too," he said casually. "Paul?" she asked, surprised. Dad hadn't told her about his brother who had died four years earlier from the same disease. Mom had no idea what muscular dystrophy was. The only thing Dad had told her about his family, trying to impress her, was that they owned a yacht back in Wisconsin. She later found out that the family yacht was actually a small fishing canoe.

After their marriage, my parents were both stationed at the Philadelphia Naval Yard. Mom was a secretary and Dad was a communications technician. A few months later, after they were both discharged, Mom became pregnant, and Dad decided they would live in Wisconsin to be closer to his family. They moved in with Dad's parents while their first home was being built. My older sister Kimberly (called Kim) was born on June 9, 1957 in Madison, Wisconsin. She was baptized by Grandfather William's brother Norman, a monsignor in the Catholic church.

CHAPTER 4

Always Moving

Mom and Dad moved into a small, new home in Madison. While Mom learned how to take care of my newborn sister, Dad worked at Sears until someone noticed how charismatic he was with customers and suggested he'd be a terrific salesman. Dad took that advice and embarked on a new career.

In the decades that followed, he excelled at sales in the burgeoning field of telecommunications. His career took our family from Madison, to Jefferson City, Missouri (where I was born) to Morehead, Minnesota, Overland Park, Kansas, Sommerville, New Jersey, Atlanta, Georgia, and Dekalb, Illinois.

The constant moves were hard on Mom who had to pack and unpack all our belongings, as well as us, without any family or friends nearby to help. She hand-carried medical records to new doctors and school records to new districts to enroll us in classes. Moving was hard for us kids too. Just as we made new friends and adjusted to our new schools, our lives would be uprooted again.

CHAPTER 5

The Rhythm Method

WHILE STILL LIVING IN MADISON, MY YOUNG married parents had my brother Mark on September 13, 1959. Mark, like Kim, was supposed to be baptized by Monsignor Thomas, but the monsignor died of a heart attack a few weeks before Mark was born.

My mother became pregnant again in 1960, but the baby was stillborn. She rationalized that God must have spared her from having a child born with muscular dystrophy. She did not want to risk another pregnancy, so she turned to her priest for guidance.

Since using birth control was not allowed by the Catholic Church, most women were advised to use the rhythm method to avoid unwanted pregnancies. It required them to track their menstrual cycles on the calendar each month to predict ovulation and the dates most likely for conception. If you didn't want to conceive, you had to avoid sex on the days you were most fertile. Menstrual cycles and the ability to keep accurate records, however, often vary. Today, the rhythm method is considered one of the least effective forms of birth control according to the Mayo Clinic.

Despite her careful planning, she became pregnant again in May 1961. My due date was February 2, 1962.

During her pregnancy, Dad's sales career took our family to Jefferson City, Missouri where my parents enjoyed being active in the United States Junior Chamber, called the Jaycees, a civic organization for young adults between the ages of 18 and 40.

On December 18, 1961 my parents were at a Jaycee dinner when Mom, wearing a new cranberry dress, felt a trickle of water during dinner. In the ladies' room she thought, "What's going on? It's too early for my water to break." Back home, she told Dad about what had happened. "Just go to sleep," he urged her, unconcerned. Later that night she started having cramps. When she called her doctor the next morning, he said not to worry. But her cramps only got worse. Now, frantic, Mom insisted on going to the hospital.

When she arrived, she was admitted and given medicine to stop labor. As my mother recalled, her doctor repeated, "Don't worry mother. Everyone gets excited around the holidays."

Over the next two days, Mom fretted, "It's too early for the baby to come," nightmares of her stillbirth flashing back. The drugs couldn't delay my premature birth. On Thursday, December 21 at 12:25 p.m., I was delivered six weeks early.

The doctor and nurses looked at me and shook their heads. They had never seen a baby so small survive and held no hope for me. Mom panicked when she didn't hear me cry. "Please don't give up. Please keep trying," she pleaded. Finally, I took my first breath and cried, and Mom cried with me. It was the first of many fights we would win together.

PART TWO:

Step By Step

CHAPTER 6

Fighting To Live

I DROPPED FIVE OUNCES FROM MY BIRTH WEIGHT of 2 pounds, 11 ounces. Since my lungs were not fully developed, I struggled to breathe and often would stop breathing entirely during cyanotic or "blue" spells when the reduced amount of blood reaching my lungs caused my skin to turn blue.

On December 23, Mom was forced to leave me behind in the hospital to make the obligatory trip to Madison to celebrate Christmas with Dad's family. Devastated to be 400 miles away from me, she put on a brave face for Kim and Mark who were excitedly waiting for Santa. In private, she'd go into the bathroom and cry, not knowing whether I'd still be alive when she returned home. "There's nothing you can do. It's in God's hands," said Mom and Pop Thomas in a futile effort to comfort her.

Even back home, she could only visit me when Dad wasn't using the car for work. I couldn't go home with her until I weighed at least five pounds. The doctors told Mom that I almost died several times during those first few weeks. "It wasn't like it is today," Mom recalled recently. "Now, they let parents in those neonatal units hold their babies. All they would let me do is look at you through glass. As soon as I got back in the car, I cried all the way home." I can still hear her pain 58 years later.

On February 21, 1962, the story of my "Life Fight..." was published in the Jefferson City *Post-Tribune*, announcing that I had just been released from the hospital. It ended with, "So, though she may not be eligible for a cake with two candles on it, Sheri certainly deserves to celebrate her second (month) birthday today." A later edition of the paper had a picture of my sister Kim and my brother Mark, ages 5 and 3, along with a caption that read, "They are all smiles about their baby sister."

Newspaper cover story about me, "Two-Pound Baby Wins Life Fight," (under picture of nurse) published on February 21, 1962.

CHAPTER 7

Sleepless Nights

Mom was elated to have me home, but every-two-hour feedings and diaper changes proved challenging. She didn't understand why I was stiff as a board when she tried to hold me or why I gagged when she bottle-fed me, as was recommended in those days, or why it was so hard to spread my tiny crossed legs apart to change my diaper.

I continued to have cyanotic spells where I would turn "blue." In her unpublished story, "Step by Step," Mom wrote, "During these episodes as I tensely awaited the return of her rhythmic breathing, I anxiously held my breath as well. I was unable to relax, even when she was sleeping, and was afraid to leave her alone. I ran on sheer nervous energy those first several weeks.

"After several months, I began to realize that Sheri wasn't responding as my other children had when they were babies. She didn't try to grasp things or even turn over. She seemed to cry easily, and usually unnecessarily, and I was very concerned because she refused to eat baby food."

When she raised these concerns with her doctor, he was unfazed. He told her he "was quite confident that since she had such a slow start, she would naturally do things slower than other children for the first year or so."

"Kim and Mark had crawled by nine months. When she wasn't crawling by that time," Mom wrote, "I became even more concerned because she didn't seem to be making any progress at all. She was not sitting up or creeping, and she still cried frequently and seemed to stiffen up, rather than relax, when I tried to comfort her. I was very frustrated because she refused to eat junior food [baby food that is slightly coarser than strained baby food] and couldn't seem to chew any solid substances."

After my christening in July 1962 we moved to Moorhead, Minnesota, just minutes from Fargo, North Dakota. The sparsely populated town was marked by brutally long, cold winters.

As the cold months rolled on, I still couldn't crawl. Instead, I pushed myself on the ground like a snake toward whatever caught my attention—or to get attention—especially from my older siblings. I would slither excitedly toward Kim and Mark and bite their ankles hoping they'd play with me. Instead, they shrieked, crying to Mom to make me stop.

I couldn't sit or stand. I also couldn't keep my stiff little hands together. When Mom tried to take a picture of me praying with Kim and Mark for our family Christmas card, she solved the problem by clasping my tiny hands together with a rubber band. In one of my favorite childhood photos, Kim and Mark are reverentially praying while I, instead, look straight at the camera.

My grandparents continued to say, "She has muscular dystrophy like Paul and Mary Ann. It's God's will." Mom had no one else to turn to. She didn't want to worry her mother back in New Jersey, and she had not yet made friends in this new, cold city.

When I was 15 months old, my parents took me to a new doctor in Fargo. After a lengthy examination, Mom wrote, "The doctor informed us that Sheri was mentally retarded,* and that she was too young to determine how much brain damage she had. He said when she got older, she could be tested to see if she could be trained in special schools or would need to be institutionalized.

"On the way home from the doctor's office my husband tried to comfort me, but I was too stunned to speak or even cry. I kept telling myself the doctor had to be wrong, that this couldn't possibly be happening to us, not after the 'miracle' of Sheri's birth." Mom's story continued, "I can't begin to describe the total despair I experienced as I spent a sleepless night trying to accept what seemed inevitable and praying for strength and direction.

"The next morning as I was feeding Sheri, her dark eyes seemed to be imploring me to help her.

I felt instinctively sure that she couldn't really be mentally retarded, and I became determined to do everything humanly possible to see exactly what she was capable of doing."

During my childhood, certain words, no longer acceptable today, were commonly used to label me and others with disabilities: "mentally retarded, crippled, and handicapped." For accuracy, I have included them, although it pains me to do so.

CHAPTER 8

Patterning

Mom thought back to an article she had read in the doctor's office a few days earlier about the benefits of cross-patterning for child development. Cross-patterning, it said, involved using the opposite arm and the opposite leg at the same time through crawling, which helped babies integrate both sides of their brain for optimum learning and development. One paragraph, about the role cross-patterning played in eye development, intrigued her since my eyes were severely cross-eyed. It said that crawling helps a child focus and refocus their eyes as they looked at the person or object they were crawling to.

Armed with this information, Mom was determined to make me crawl to "uncross" my eyes. After feeding me that morning, she tied an empty ice cream carton around my belly in order to put me into a crawling position. She would kneel in front of me and dangle my favorite toy just out of reach as she implored me to come get it.

After trying for a few seconds to reach my toy in this new, unfamiliar position, I would roll over onto my back like a turtle and cry furiously. Over and over again, Mom would flip me back onto my belly and dangle another toy in front of me, only to have me roll over again in frustration.

We were both fiercely determined. She wanted me to crawl as much as I wanted my toy. After days of trying, I finally figured out how to use my arms and legs to crawl toward my toy. Crawling helped my eyes focus and slowly straighten out. I still had a lazy right eye, but my eyes weren't nearly as crossed as they had been. Forty years later, I had successful strabismus surgery to straighten my wandering right eye.

Teaching me to crawl convinced Mom that I could do even more. As she wrote, "Through perseverance and determination, I taught her to sit up, eat table food, feed herself, and I even began to potty train her. She responded very slowly, but she *did respond*, and to me this was a sign she could learn.

"My biggest worry was still the fact that she couldn't pull herself up to a standing position, and when we tried to support her in this position, her legs seemed to buckle. I discussed this with the doctor several times and his reply was always the same, 'This is just one of the many problems you can expect from a mentally retarded child.'"

Dad seemed unconcerned. He had seen his own mother raise two children with muscular dystrophy, and he expected Mom to do the same. The more my grandparents and Dad continued to say

I had muscular dystrophy, and the more the doctors called me mentally retarded, the more Mom refused to believe it.

As I read her words 50 years later, I realize how extraordinary Mom's determination and perseverance were. She could have given up after she heard the words "mentally retarded" and relegated me to a life of low expectations and achievements. Instead, her decision to fight for me changed the course of my life.

Mom tries to keep me upright.

CHAPTER 9

The Yellow Pages

MOM DIDN'T KNOW IF SHE WAS DOING "the right things for and with me," and she didn't know where to go for help. By the time I was a toddler, in desperation, she picked up the Yellow Pages and started calling county agencies before finally reaching the welfare office. Hearing the urgency in her voice, someone promised her they would send a county health nurse to visit us the following week. After she hung up the phone, she cried with relief because finally someone was coming to help us.

A few days later, after Dad left for work and Kim and Mark caught the school bus, a young visiting nurse knocked on our door, and Mom eagerly let her in. She examined me and asked Mom questions. "It was the first time I had talked to someone else in depth about you, and it was the first time someone had really listened to my concerns," recalled Mom during a recent phone conversation.

The nurse didn't know what was wrong with me, but she could hear the pleading in Mom's voice. She said there was a clinic in Minneapolis four hours away that might be able to diagnose me, and an appointment was made to have me tested. I think the clinic she referred Mom to was the Mayo Clinic, but I don't have any medical records to verify this.

Dad resisted the idea of getting me tested since he thought I had muscular dystrophy and that nothing could be done. Since I was scheduled for two days of testing, it also meant he would have to miss a few days of work, losing money our family couldn't afford to lose.

When he saw how determined Mom was, he reluctantly made arrangements. My parents left Kim and Mark with neighbors they barely knew, and since hotels were too expensive, they stayed with a friend of a friend in Minneapolis they had never met while I stayed overnight at the hospital.

I was thoroughly x-rayed and tested by a team of doctors. They evaluated my motor skills, muscle tone, reflexes, posture and communication skills. At the end of the second day, the head doctor told my parents I had "mild, spastic cerebral palsy." They said I was fortunate in that it primarily affected my legs and feet and not my whole body. The doctor explained that spastic cerebral palsy made my leg muscles too stiff for me to stand or walk properly without corrective treatment.

The doctors patiently answered my parents many questions and told them what could be surgically done for a child with cerebral palsy. They also referred my parents to an orthopedist associated with the state "crippled children's commission."

As Mom wrote, "When I expressed my fears about her mentality, they assured me they were confident from the test results that she was not mentally retarded. Now that I was reassured that Sheri was not mentally retarded and that my instincts hadn't failed me, I felt my confidence returning, instilling an inner strength which I knew would be necessary to see us through uncertain future ordeals."

CHAPTER 10

CP

"Cerebral Palsy (CP) affects a person's ability to move and maintain balance and posture and is the most common motor disability in childhood, affecting 1 in 323 children. Most (75% to 85%) children with CP have spastic CP which means that their muscles are stiff, and as a result, their movements can be awkward. Over half of children with CP can walk independently," according to the Centers for Disease Control and Prevention (CDC). "Most CP is related to brain damage that happened before or during birth and is called congenital CP." The CDC has also identified certain risk factors that increase the chance that a child will have cerebral palsy. Two of them include premature birth (I was born six weeks early) and a low birthweight (I weighed only 2 pounds, 11 ounces).

Many people with CP, like my cousin Buster, use wheelchairs or walkers, and/or all their limbs and speech are affected.

According to the Cerebral Palsy Alliance, one in four people with cerebral palsy cannot talk, and others, "have difficulty controlling their movement enough to produce speech that is clear and understood by others." Most people mistake a person's inability to speak or their garbled speech as a sign of an intellectual disability.

According to the Cerebral Palsy Guidance website, "around 764,000 people in the U.S. (including adults and children) have at least one symptom of cerebral palsy." For more information or to find out about services and community support in your area, visit www.ucp.org.

CHAPTER 11

The Slide

During my childhood, "crippled" was the word most people used to categorize me and other children with disabilities, especially in official documents and legislation. "State crippled children's programs had their origin in the Social Security Act of 1935." Social Security amendments in 1965 provided states with funding to pay for care, and for operations, for children in "medically indigent families." At the time, "a crippled child was an orthopedically handicapped child," which qualified me. Since my parents had little money, I also qualified as "medically indigent." Today, the program has been expanded to cover children with all types of disabilities.

A few months after I was diagnosed with cerebral palsy, we moved to Overland Park, Kansas, 20 minutes from Kansas City, Kansas, where Mom took me to my initial appointment at the Crippled Children's Commission. After a team of orthopedists examined me, I was measured for lower leg braces with leather straps and steel rods attached to heavy, thick-soled orthopedic shoes. After the braces arrived and I was strapped into them, I was encouraged to take my first awkward steps.

As Mom wrote, "She sustained many hard falls but always picked herself up quickly, laughed at our concerned expressions, and continued playing. I also took her twice weekly to a physical therapist for exercises to strengthen her leg muscles which I repeated every night before she went to bed. She accepted this way of life cheerfully, and her determination made things so much easier for all of us." As a small child, I learned to how to please my parents, the doctors and everyone else around me: always smile and never complain.

Over the next few years, I would be fitted for new braces as I grew. I spent most of the next several months dragging legs laden with heavy braces up and down the staircases in our many homes, built decades before accessible housing was even an option. I can still remember how heavy and uncomfortable those braces were. To me, they felt like inescapable weights tethering my tiny, painfully thin legs to the ground as I tried to lift my feet to walk.

At the playground, I desperately wanted to slide down the slide like all the other children. On a chilly October day just before I turned three, I tried over and over again to climb the ladder with my heavy leg braces, only to face frustration at the top because I couldn't swing my legs over the last rung.

I kept trying for almost two hours as my legs grew weary and darkness approached. Having watched me struggle long enough, Mom finally came over and pleaded, "Come on, Sheri. It's time to go home."

Now, I became frantic to slide down the slide before she could stop me. Summoning all my dwindling strength, I made one last attempt to swing my legs over the top of the ladder. Success! I was finally on the other side ready to slide down to Mom who was anxiously waiting for me at the bottom. Mom said my smile was as big as a Cheshire cat. That fall day, I learned about the power of perseverance. And I owe that important lesson to my mother, who could have easily lifted me onto the slide, but instead allowed me to find my own way and discover my own ability.

I'm wearing my first pair of braces during a visit to New Jersey in the early 1960s. Left to right: Grandmom Noami, Uncle Eddie (holding me) and Mom.

CHAPTER 12

Operations

IN DECEMBER 1964, THE WEEK BEFORE I TURNED three, I had the first of many orthopedic surgeries on my legs and feet. After months of wearing leg braces, I was still struggling to walk, and doctors determined that I needed a series of operations to improve my mobility by loosening the tight, spastic muscles in my legs. The first operation loosened the hamstring muscles running up the back of my legs.

"After the casts came off," Mom wrote, "she wore the braces only at night, and the improvement in her walking was quite noticeable. She was as proud of her progress as we were, but we knew that she had a long way to go. She had a remarkable disposition and seemed capable of adapting to almost any situation. Mentally, she was as alert as other children her age."

During the day, instead of braces, I was now able to wear white orthopedic high-top shoes which delighted me because they were much lighter to maneuver.

When I was four, Mom enrolled me briefly at a "crippled children's" nursery school, which I hated because many of the other children seemed so much more disabled than I was.

After every operation, I was in casts for three or four months. When the initial casts came off after six to eight weeks, I would be fitted with walking casts, which were plaster casts covering my feet and lower legs up to the knee with rubber stoppers on the bottom so I could walk. All I could see were my toes, which I spent endless hours wiggling. I would wear my walking casts for another six to eight weeks, followed by weeks of intensive physical therapy to strengthen my atrophied muscles. Today, walking casts have been replaced by air cast boots with comfortable padding.

Over the next two years I would have heel cord release surgery on both feet and, around age four, my most traumatic surgery of all: an operation to fix my hip sockets and release the tight muscles that made my legs "scissor" which describes how my knees and feet got tangled up, one behind the other, when I tried walk.

When I woke up from this surgery, I was in a cast up to my waist with my legs spread apart with a 2x4 piece of wood plastered between them. For the next two months, as I recovered at home in this bulky cast, I couldn't sit in a chair or on the couch or really do much of anything. Mom put a small mattress on the floor and propped me up on it to watch television. Being immobile and unable to play outside was torture. To carry me around, she held on to the 2x4 between my legs while I put my arms around her neck.

Before the surgery, I had just started to wear pretty regular panties, which I was very proud of. Now, they wouldn't fit over this bulky cast, and Mom had no choice but to put me back in diapers temporarily. "I don't want to wear diapers. I want my panties," I cried angrily, to no avail.

Mom saved two pictures of me recovering at home. One is of Mark and Kim sitting on the floor next to my mattress with me lying in the middle covered with a blanket to hide my cast, our poodle Pepe at my feet. The other one is taken on Halloween with all three of us wearing masks and holding bags of candy. Mom had taken some of their trick-or-treat candy to fill my empty bag. A mask covers my sadness at being stuck in bed while my sister and brother happily trick-or-treated.

Mom and Pop Thomas still wanted us to celebrate Christmas back in Madison. Since I couldn't ride in the car with my spread-eagle leg casts, Pop Thomas sent the REA plane to fly us back to Madison. Kim, Mark and I were excited to take our first plane ride. When the pilot, Art Anderson, saw my casted body he recoiled in shock, "She can't ride in the plane. She won't fit in a seat." Mom said, "Don't worry," as she carried me into the plane and placed me in the middle of the aisle, where I happily sat on the floor all the way to Madison.

A few weeks later, doctors removed my casts with the dreaded cast saw. A cast saw is an oscillating power tool with a small-toothed blade that rapidly vibrates back and forth to cut through plaster. As I sat on the examining table, I clung to Mom and cried hysterically as the cast saw came to life, terrified the loud, whirring blades would cut right through my tiny, thin legs. When the scary saw was turned off, doctors used a cast spreader to loosen the casts before removing them. Once the casts were off, I could finally stop crying.

While we lived in Overland Park, Kansas, I made a radio commercial to support the 'Crippled' Children's Commission. I don't remember what I said, but I remember being chosen because I had a clear speaking voice, unlike other children with cerebral palsy whose speech was affected.

42 IMBALANCED

Recovering at home at age 4 after an operation to repair my hip sockets, surrounded by my sister Kim, my brother Mark and our poodle Pepe. I'm lying on a mattress Mom set up in the living room with a blanket covering my full body cast.

CHAPTER 13

Just Like All The Other Children

IN SEPTEMBER 1967, WHEN I WAS 5½, MOM WENT to enroll me in kindergarten at our neighborhood school in Overland Park, Kansas. Since I was so independent and determined, Mom didn't foresee any problems. Instead, school officials were reluctant to admit me and suggested that I would be better off in a 'crippled' children's school. Mom was furious, "There's nothing wrong with her mentally. She can do everything the other children do. There may be some things she can't do on the playground, but she'll let you know."

The principal responded, "But how will she open a door or go to the bathroom?" "Just like all the other children," Mom angrily replied.

Mom won her argument, and I started school the next day.

Luckily, Mom saved my kindergarten report card filled out by my teacher, Mrs. Doris Jean Watson. She noted that I knew "numbers one to ten" very well, which makes me laugh, because after kindergarten, my number skills deserted me, and math became my worst subject.

She checked off that I did almost all the other skills "reasonably well," except for art, where I was "very poor in developing muscular coordination and control in using crayons, pencils and scissors. I'm sure she's trying her best," wrote Mrs. Watson. Thankfully, none of my early artwork survived, so I'll take her word for it.

On the back of the report card, Mrs. Watson wrote words that make me cry as I read them 50 years later. I'm sure, at the time, they made Mom cry too. She wrote, "It has added to my enjoyment of life knowing her."

The problem was that other children didn't want to take the time to get to know me like my teacher did. They were scared of me because I was different, and they wouldn't play with me. I felt alone even though I was surrounded by other children. On the top of the report card next to 'plays and works well with other children' Mrs. Watson checked 'seldom.' She wrote, "This was hard to check for Sheri. She has long spells of playing entirely by herself."

As Mom wrote in her unpublished story, "There are far deeper scars than those left by the surgeon's knife that Sheri has learned to contend with. Loneliness and a lack of acceptance has proved painful and disappointing to Sheri, but her outgoing personality has helped her compensate somewhat. The loneliness of a handicapped child is difficult to convey, and sadly, solitude sometimes is their only companion."

Books, records, and TV eased my solitude. I read all the Nancy Drew mysteries and dreamed I could climb "The Hidden Staircase" just like Nancy. For Christmas one year, I got the huge hardcover *Guinness World Records* book and devoured it, fascinated by all the pictures of different people, like the man with the world's longest beard and the world's tallest man. In this book, people were celebrated for being different and called record holders. I wanted to be a record holder like them instead of being shunned because I was different.

I spent Saturday afternoons listening to albums and small 45s on my record player. I loved *The Jackson 5* with Michael Jackson, and later Elton John with his outrageous glasses. Behind my closed bedroom door, I could happily dance in private instead of being made fun of in public.

My two favorite TV shows were *The Brady Bunch* and *The Waltons* because they depicted loving parents and happy kids. In our home, my parents fought, my father yelled and Kim, Mark and I could barely stand one another.

CHAPTER 14

Rudolph

Mom thought that I got short-changed every year because my birthday was only four days before Christmas. She urged me to celebrate by birthday in July so it would get the attention it deserved. When I resisted, she tried her best to make my birthday special by making a cake decorated in pink, rather than Christmas green and red, and wrapping my gifts in colorful birthday paper instead of extra Christmas wrapping paper.

I loved celebrating my birthday in December because I loved everything about Christmas, including all the holiday specials on TV. My favorite was *Rudolph the Red-Nosed Reindeer*, which first aired on NBC in 1964.

At the end of the animated classic, Burl Ives sings its signature song. The lyrics resonated with me because, like Rudolph, I was ostracized for the way I looked. He was made fun of because he had a red nose which made him different from all the other reindeer. I was made fun of, and called horrible names like "retard" and "crippled," because I had cerebral palsy and walked differently.

Every Christmas, I couldn't wait to sing my favorite song. I thought the words were written just for me, to let me know that I could shine like Rudolph.

CHAPTER 15

Another Beer

As I look back 50 years later, I marvel at how Mom was able to care for Kim, Mark and a daughter with cerebral palsy essentially all by herself. Dad's sales career took him away from home Monday through Friday, and even on weekends, he expected Mom to take care of him and us children so that he could be left alone to drink his beer and watch sports.

When he was home, Dad's favorite saying was "Hey Sheri, go get Dad another beer." As a small girl wanting to please her Daddy, I happily went to get him another beer. I didn't know that he was an alcoholic and that his drinking fueled the anger that permeated our home.

During the week, whenever we caused trouble, Mom would threaten us with, "Wait until your father comes home." As soon as Dad walked in the door on Friday night, Mom was ready with her list of everything we had done wrong during the week. Kim, Mark and I, on the other hand, couldn't wait to tell Daddy what we had done in school during the week and show him all our artwork. All of us pouncing on him at once, after he'd been away all week, overwhelmed his initial happiness at seeing us. After a quick dinner, Dad would start his weekend drinking binge.

One moment Dad would be laughing and playing with us, and the next moment he would be screaming at Mom or us with a terrifying rage.

CHAPTER 16

Radio City Music Hall

On a bitterly cold December day in 1969, Mom took us to see the Radio City Music Hall Christmas Show in New York City. I had just turned eight. I was so excited. It was our first trip to the city, and I couldn't wait to see the colorful extravaganza.

After driving for nearly an hour and finally finding a place to park, we walked several blocks to Radio City Music Hall and found an impossibly long line waiting to be let inside. My legs were already hurting from the long walk. After about 20 minutes standing in line in the bitter cold, the muscles in my legs began to stiffen in painful spasms. I started crying softly to myself. Mom tried to comfort me by saying, "It won't be much longer. We'll be inside soon." But the line wasn't moving, and as the minutes dragged on, my pain and cries intensified.

Finally, Mom had had enough. She marched up to the front of the line and frantically waved to get the attention of a uniformed usher inside. When he opened the door, I could hear her even from where I was standing, "My daughter's handicapped, and we've been waiting in line for 45 minutes. Is there anywhere she could sit down?" Startled, the man said, "Of course, Ma'am. Just bring her and the rest of your party to me, and I'll let you inside and find your daughter a chair." Although I was finally inside, the cold had done its damage. My legs continued to spasm for most of the show, and I couldn't enjoy it.

Before that day, it had never occurred to Mom that she could ask for any type of special accommodation. When I grew up during the 1960s and '70s, no one thought about making things accessible for people with disabilities. Today, because of the Americans with Disabilities Act (ADA) and greater disability awareness, things are better but not perfect. Although the ADA (signed into law in 1990) prohibits discrimination so that people with disabilities have the same opportunities as everyone else to participate in daily activities, it isn't always enforced. We still have to fight discrimination and for employment opportunities, accessible housing, transportation and more.

Mom wasn't the only one who fought for me. One day, as I was walking home from school, a boy pushed me to the ground and said, "You retard!" loud enough for my older sister Kim to hear. She ran up to him and shouted, "How dare you call my sister that!" as she punched him in the face. Even though she got in big trouble for throwing that punch, I was delighted that she stuck up for me.

CHAPTER 17

Little Man

WHEN I WAS NINE, OUR FAMILY MOVED TO A suburb just outside of Atlanta. It was 1970. Our house's front lawn had Bermuda grass which reminded me of the putting greens at the Masters where Jack Nicklaus won so many green jackets. Our velvety-soft front lawn instantly became the favorite spot for neighborhood soccer games. The back yard had an expansive lawn that blended into the woods.

We were welcomed to the neighborhood by a friendly crow that we called Blackie. He became a daily delight, especially to Mom. Whenever she went to get the mail, Blackie would do a mating dance on top of the mailbox. He also loved to swoop down and steal her cigarettes while she tanned in the backyard or interrupt our soccer games by furiously chasing and pecking at the ball.

Our parents surprised us that summer with a Dalmatian. Kim, Mark and I named him Snoopy because his black ears reminded us of our favorite Peanuts character. We all adored him, but for me, he was much more than a pet. He was not only my best friend, he was my only friend. Snoopy was a gentle dog who loved to be cuddled, and I spent hours each day petting his soft black-spotted white coat as he listened to my stories and wagged his tail in agreement.

I loved Snoopy so much that I wrote my first poem, "Little Man," about him when I was nine years old:

> LITTLE MAN
> Little man, little man,
> I see you as you are.
> Why do people see you afar...?

When I read those words today, I realize that I wasn't just writing about Snoopy. I wanted the neighborhood kids to see me for who I was on the inside rather than judge me from afar because of what they saw on the outside.

While Snoopy ran eagerly to Mom, Kim, Mark and me for affection, he hid from Dad by cowering behind the ivory family room curtains. With just his head peeking out from under the drapes, we joked that he looked like the Virgin Mary.

Snoopy was terrified of Dad because he often bore the brunt of Dad's pent-up anger and rage. Mom shielded us from his fits of anger as best she could, but she couldn't protect Snoopy. Dad expected his male dog to exude strength and masculinity at all times. Instead, Snoopy was gentle and docile, which infuriated him.

Mom began to dream of making a fresh start for herself and her children, free of Dad's temper and unpredictable behavior. She loved Atlanta, and she thought that if she ever divorced Dad, she'd be able to stay in our house, which she had painstakingly decorated in 1970s Harvest Gold and Avocado Green. Best of all, Mom figured that she could rent out the basement to bring in some income, which she'd need since she had no job experience.

When Mom asked Kim how she wanted her Georgia bedroom decorated, my sister squealed, "lime green and purple!" So Mom set about granting her wish. She painted the walls solid lime green and dyed a white faux fur blanket dark purple for the bedspread, which she garnished with furry round smiley face pillows.

Kim, unfortunately, wouldn't have long to enjoy her new purple and lime green room. A few months after it was completed, Dad lured Mom into one last move to Dekalb County, Illinois with the promise of a big promotion and an even bigger house. Even though she didn't want to go, Mom agreed to the move in order to give her marriage, and Dad, one last shot.

As she packed for Illinois, Dad forced her to do one more thing. He told her to get rid of Snoopy because he said it'd be too hard to drive with him in the car all the way to Illinois. I don't know why Mom agreed to it. I just remember how devastated

I was when Mom told us that we couldn't take Snoopy with us. I remember her crying as she handed Snoopy over to a local farmer who agreed to take him. Just like that, our beloved dog, and my best friend, was gone.

CHAPTER 18

The Saucer

THE MOVE TO ILLINOIS DIDN'T HELP MOM AND Dad's marriage. There had been too much tension and too much yelling for too many years. I turned 11 on December 21, 1972. A few days later, Dad's parents came to Illinois to celebrate Christmas with us. Mom put on a brave face through the festivities even though she knew that she'd finally have to tell them that she was divorcing Dad, painful news to devout Catholics who viewed marriage as a sacred vow to be endured but never broken

Mom also kept the news from Kim, Mark and me. She didn't want to spoil our last Christmas together or upset me, because I was scheduled for major surgery two days after Christmas.

Blissfully unaware that my family would be broken apart a few months later, I was excited to use the new saucer sled I unwrapped Christmas morning to slide down the hill behind our house. Bundled up in my red parka and mittens, blue snow pants and boots, I slid down the icy hill several times and somehow managed to avoid the small creek at the bottom.

Finally, Mom opened the back door and yelled, "It's time to come in and get out of your snow gear and get ready for lunch." I had already dragged my saucer up to the top of the hill for another run. "Ok Mom, I'll be right in," I screamed as I took off for one final run. But this time, my saucer sled spun wildly out of control down the hill, and I realized in terror that there was no way I'd be able to stop my momentum before tumbling into the icy creek.

The next instant I was totally submerged. Kim and Mark were sledding nearby and heard me scream as I crashed into the water. They raced to the creek and pulled me and the saucer out. With herculean effort I dragged myself back home. When Mom opened the door, she was horrified to see me covered in ice and shivering. "What happened?" she screamed at Kim and Mark who were supposed to be watching me.

Mom was scared that I would catch a terrible cold which would postpone my scheduled operation. It had happened once before when I was younger. I had arrived at the hospital the day before an operation with chest congestion due to a cold. Doctors told me that it wasn't safe for me to go under anesthesia, and the operation was postponed. I was so disappointed that I cried uncontrollably right in front of Mom and the doctors.

Fortunately, I was symptom-free when I arrived at the hospital for my three-hour surgery. Back then, it was customary to be admitted to the hospital the day before surgery for pre-op tests and stay in the hospital for a few days of recovery.

Today, things are much different. In the past 15 years, I've had two brain surgeries, major toe reconstruction and kidney surgery, all done as an outpatient. You go to a hospital or local surgery center in the morning, get operated on, wake up from anesthesia, and then go home a few hours later, all in one day.

On December 27, 1972 I underwent the Grice Procedure, named after the doctor who first performed it. Somehow doctors had convinced Mom that it would be beneficial for me to have arches constructed inside my flat feet. The Grice Procedure was a long, complex surgery that involved removing a 12-inch piece of my right shinbone (tibia) from my leg and breaking it into little pieces to build an arch in each foot. When I woke up, I was in full leg casts curved at the knee so I could sit.

A few days after surgery, I was sitting in a wheelchair in my hospital room when I reached for the call button attached to my bed, causing the wheelchair to tip forward. Although my leg casts acted as a stopper to keep me from falling out of the wheelchair, all my weight was shifted onto my surgically-repaired feet, which were not supposed to bear any weight at all. I cried out hoping someone would hear me. Still, no nurses came.

Luckily, Mom heard me as she was walking toward my room and rushed in to find me precariously tilted forward in my wheelchair. She grabbed the handles of the wheelchair to sit me back upright and left me momentarily to berate the nurses outside, "How dare you leave my daughter alone crying for help!"

After I was discharged, I spent the next six weeks being carried by Mom or Dad from my bedroom to the couch to read or watch TV, and most embarrassingly, to the bathroom. When my leg casts came off, I was fitted with walking casts up to my knees, with rubber stoppers on the bottom so I could walk as my feet healed.

The night after I got my walking casts, Dad screamed at me during dinner for seemingly no reason. Terrified, I got up from the table and tried to walk away from him, barely able to put weight on my surgically-repaired feet. Unbelievably, he started chasing me. I tried to run as best I could. I desperately wanted to get to my bedroom and lock the door so that I'd be safe from Dad's rage. Fortunately, I got there just in time.

CHAPTER 19

We're Getting Divorced

As soon as my walking casts came off, Mom and Dad sat us down and said, "We're getting divorced." Mom felt that Kim and Mark (now 16 and 13) were old enough to decide who they wanted to live with. Kim and I went to live with Mom, and Mark, who felt sorry for Dad, decided to live with him.

They moved back to Georgia. Dad focused on dating rather than parenting, leaving Mark to fend for himself. It was hard on my brother, and Mom would regret that she let a 13-year-old Mark make the decision to live with him.

Mom decided to move back to New Jersey so she'd be close to her family for emotional support. We lived in an apartment complex in South Jersey, not far from Grandmother Naomi's house in Mt. Holly. Even though Mom had never really worked, outside of her short stint doing secretarial work in the Navy, she needed a job to support us. She eventually found administrative work with a company that provided home health care nurses.

Dad was supposed to pay child support, but after just a few payments, he stopped. Mom periodically tried to go to court to force Dad to pay child support, but he moved so often it was hard to track him down. So we were on our own financially.

CHAPTER 20

Living In a Normal World

MOM DESPERATELY WANTED ME TO BE ACCEPTED in the "normal" world so she sought to mitigate other more noticeable side effects of my cerebral palsy by constantly correcting me. For example, when I was excited, I would make contorted faces that I was unaware of. "Stop making faces!" Mom implored. At other times, my mouth would slack open and she'd say, "Stop letting the flies in."

She thought her rebukes would get me to stop making faces. Eventually, they did. But as a budding teenager, her constant criticism stung and confused me and made me feel sorry for myself when I looked at all the seemingly perfect students around me.

So Mom arranged for me to be a summer camp counselor at a day camp for children with severe disabilities, including cerebral palsy. Most of the kids needed 24-hour care and couldn't walk or feed themselves. It was a real wake-up call, and I never felt sorry for myself again. The local cerebral palsy center and the camp were run by Virginia Alwine, who had CP herself. It was the first time I had ever seen someone with CP in a leadership position.

Today, as I look back on that painful time, I can understand what motivated Mom. She thought the best way to love me was to constantly push and prod me. Now, I'm glad she "encouraged" me to reach my full potential, to become the woman I am today.

CHAPTER 21

Jaguar

WHEN I WAS ABOUT 13, SHORTLY AFTER I STARTED menstruating, I developed another serious health problem that still plagues me. On top of everything else I was dealing with, I started getting piercing headaches above my left eye that felt like I was being stabbed by a million knives. The headaches were unbearable, and when the pain intensified I often reflexively vomited.

I didn't know what triggered these violent headaches which seemingly came on without warning. When I asked Mom about them, she said they were sinus headaches and that she suffered from them too. She gave me some of her sinus medicine to keep in my purse and told me to take it at the first sign of a headache. Sometimes I remembered to take the medicine right away, and the headache would go away after an hour or so. Other times, I thought I could tough it out without having to take the sinus medicine, which I hated because it made me drowsy. But the pain would become so unbearable that I'd have to take twice as much to get any relief.

One day, when I was about 14, Mom and I were riding with Aunt Roberta in her new Jaguar when a headache came on. I had left my purse at home, so I had no medicine with me to alleviate it. As we drove in city traffic, the pain got so severe that I vomited all over myself, Mom and the interior of the Jaguar. I never forgot my medicine again.

PART THREE:
The Write Stuff

CHAPTER 22

Watergate

When I was a kid, eccentric Aunt Roberta always wrapped our Christmas gifts in newspaper comics, and we didn't receive them until months later. She celebrated Christmas in July, years before retailers started promoting it to increase summer sales.

After delighting in my poem "Little Man," which she had the art department at her advertising agency print and frame, she continued to encourage my writing and budding interest in journalism by giving me books by famous writers and newspaper columnists like Ellen Goodman.

I devoured the books and dreamed of becoming a famous journalist, especially after I read *All the President's Men* by Bob Woodward and Carl Bernstein, the two Washington Post reporters who broke open the Watergate scandal that resulted in President Nixon's resignation in 1974.

I read the newspaper every day and watched the evening news with Walter Cronkite every night. I never missed an episode of *60 Minutes* and loved watching Dan Rather expose scandal after scandal.

Today, I worry that kids aren't being taught about the important role journalists play in holding our public officials accountable and exposing corruption. News has become more about entertainment than information, making it difficult to distinguish real news from fake news.

While Watergate was unfolding, Mom met John Carmany, a burly bearded man who worked for the post office. After a brief courtship, they married. Mom thought, after her turbulent marriage to Dad, that she had finally found true happiness. So she was devastated when, after 10 years together, she discovered that John was having an affair with a woman who worked at his post office. After she divorced him, it took her a long time to recover emotionally. In the early '90s, she met, fell in love, and married Domenick Smedile (who we called Dom), a wonderful caring man who she was happily married to until his death in 2019.

CHAPTER 23

Chimera

IN 1977, I STARTED 10TH GRADE AT A BRAND-new high school in the racially diverse William Levitt-planned community of Willingboro, New Jersey. We moved there because the homes were relatively inexpensive. I became friends with students of all races and cultures and learned that we were more alike than different.

At Willingboro High School, I immediately set about starting my career in journalism by joining the newspaper staff of the *Chimera Chronicle*, headed by teacher Marie Plavin, a kindly ex nun.

"What was a Chimera anyway," I wondered. I soon found out that a chimera (first syllable pronounced like the beginning of kite) is a mythological fire-breathing female monster with a lion's head, a goat's body, and a serpent's tail.

When I joined the school newspaper, I volunteered to cover sports. Watching football with Dad years before had turned me into a sports junkie. Boys didn't expect a girl to know much about sports, so I loved to astound them with my encyclopedic knowledge about players, teams and statistics. Whenever I saw a group of guys talking about sports, I would interrupt and say, "What about so and so? ... Did you know he rushed for ... last season?" They would stare at me as I kept right on talking.

I became the first female sports editor of the *Chimera Chronicle* the following year. I wish I had pursued a career in sports journalism. My family always said I would have made a great sports announcer. Every time I see a female sports announcer on TV, I wonder what could have been.

As sports editor, in addition to football and basketball, I loved covering track and field. Carl Lewis, the future track and field legend who would go on to win nine gold medals in four Olympic games starting in 1984, was the star of our high school track team, along with his sister Carol. They were coached by their mother Evelyn Lewis who had been a track star in her own right in the 1950s. Carl Lewis would have won even more gold medals if he had been allowed to compete in the 1980 Olympics in Moscow, which were boycotted by the U.S. to protest the Soviet invasion of Afghanistan.

Since I spent so many hours hanging around the track, Mrs. Lewis asked me if I wanted to become a manager for the team. I was thrilled. I would be able to travel with the team to all the track meets, and I would be able to wear a cool track team warm-up jacket just like the rest of the team. Imagine me, a kid called "crippled" managing the track team. I readily agreed, and Mrs. Lewis said she would call Mom to OK it with her.

I eagerly anticipated her call later that night; I was sure Mom wouldn't have a problem with me joining just one more school activity. I was already envisioning how good I'd look in the warm-up jacket. For me, it was an opportunity to look like a real athlete, which I knew I would have been if it weren't for my cerebral palsy.

When Mrs. Lewis called, my heart sank as I heard Mom's voice. "Oh, Mrs. Lewis, so nice of you to call. …Oh, I see. Thank you for thinking of Sheri. She's got so much on her plate now. She's got her schoolwork and she's got the newspaper. I just don't think that she can take on one more thing." And just like that, my dream of being the track team manager ended when Mom hung up the phone.

I was devastated. It was my biggest disappointment in high school. Although I continued to cover Carl Lewis as sports editor, my joy in covering the track team dissipated.

In the 1970s, students with disabilities were excluded from competing in high school athletics. Today, thanks to the efforts of Paralympian Tatyana McFadden, things are different for students with disabilities.

I met Tatyana in 2004 when I was a member of the Howard County Commission on Disabilities and she was being honored as our Youth Award Winner. She was born in Russia with spina bifida and spent the first six years of her life in an orphanage. Without a wheelchair, Tatyana learned to get around by walking on her hands. She was adopted by Deborah McFadden, a Howard County resident who had traveled to Russia as Commissioner of Disabilities for the U.S. Department of Health.

Deborah McFadden enrolled Tatyana in youth sports to strengthen her upper body. When she was in high school, Tatyana and her mother filed a lawsuit against the Howard County school system to allow Tatyana to compete with her fellow students. U.S. District Court judge Andre Davis stated, "She's not suing for blue ribbons, gold ribbons, or money—she just wants to be out there when everyone else is out there."

The lawsuit led to the passage of the Maryland Fitness and Athletics Equity for Students with Disabilities Act, requiring schools to give students with disabilities the opportunity to compete in interscholastic athletics. In 2013, the Obama administration passed the Sports and Fitness Equity Law, nicknamed Tatyana's Law, modeled after the Maryland legislation she helped pass.

Tatyana went on to win numerous Paralympic medals in wheelchair racing and several marathons around the world. She's even been featured in television commercials, something previously unheard of for people with disabilities. Today, even when TV shows and movies feature characters with disabilities, they are overwhelmingly portrayed by non-disabled actors, something advocates are working hard to change.

In September 2020, Tatyana starred in and produced *Rising Phoenix*, a documentary about extraordinary Paralympic athletes and how the Paralympics have impacted global disability awareness.

In a recent newspaper article, Tatyana said, "I love sharing my story, especially with the young. Hopefully, we can change people's perspectives on what disability is; how it's our character that gets us to where we are and not what we look like."

CHAPTER 24

Stretching

My senior year in high school, 1979, was a pivotal year for me. I was named Editor-in-Chief of the *Chimera Chronicle,* which won an award from the Columbia Scholastic Press Association, and I met Douglas Spandau.

During gym class in October, our teacher instructed us to find a partner for stretching exercises. Just as I had resigned myself to stretching alone, a slender boy with long wavy blonde hair came over to me and smiled, "Can I be your partner?" Relieved, I smiled back, "Sure!" And just like that, I met the love of my life. We've been together ever since. Thank God for stretching exercises!

With his wavy blond hair and mustache, I thought he looked just like my favorite basketball player, Larry Bird of the Boston Celtics.

The next day, Doug asked me if he could walk me home from school. I readily agreed. He carried my heavy books while I snuck glances at his angular face and kind blue eyes. For him, it was love at first sight. I was just thrilled to have a boy, any boy, walk me home. Within a few days, we were boyfriend and girlfriend. Wow! I actually had a boyfriend! I don't know who was more thrilled, me or Mom.

Doug and I at my senior prom in 1980.

CHAPTER 25

Meet The Spandaus

Mom began inviting Doug to celebrate Thanksgiving and Christmas with us, and she always gave him the big drumsticks from our holiday turkeys, which he happily devoured. Doug was Jewish and his family celebrated Hanukkah, but he also loved celebrating Christmas with us.

Going to Doug's house was another matter entirely. His mother, Eleanor, was mentally erratic and often talked incoherently about several topics at the same time. She never cleaned the house, and Doug was constantly throwing out food that had gone rotten in the refrigerator. She also left most of the cooking to Doug, even though he had a brother, Leslie, who was five years older.

I was afraid to eat anything in Doug's house. Whenever I visited, I would signal to Doug as soon as I could that it was time for us all to head to the local diner. It was better to eat with his family in public rather than risk eating any of the food in Eleanor's refrigerator.

Doug's father, Irwin, was a World War II hero who landed at Normandy and later helped liberate the Buchenwald concentration camp at the end of the war. He took hundreds of pictures which he brought out to show me every time I came to visit.

During the war, he was hospitalized briefly for shell shock, and after he came home, he constantly relived the wartime battles that defined him. He had kept a war-time diary, and Doug and I helped him self-publish his book, *Lost Diary: A True War Story*, six years before his death in 1999.

Doug idolized his father and shared his even disposition. He followed in his father's footsteps and joined the Army after he graduated from high school, a year after me, in 1981.

He was trained as an air traffic controller and served eight years, followed by two years in the National Guard. His Army experience paved the way for his current career as an aviation systems analyst.

Doug's brother Leslie developed schizophrenia in his early 20s. He lived aimlessly at home with his parents until his mid-40s, when he was arrested after attacking Eleanor during a psychotic episode. He was court-ordered to live at a group home, where his medication was administered by injection, since he refused to take oral medication on his own.

Doug would visit him from time to time and buy him clothes. The group home was rundown and poorly staffed. Leslie spent his days chain smoking. One day in 2012, a staff member called to say that he had been diagnosed with lung cancer that had spread throughout his body and didn't have long to live. Doug visited Leslie one last time at the hospice center where he had been transferred. He died three weeks later on Doug's birthday, March 11.

Eleanor lived alone in squalor for another 10 years, refusing all our offers of help. She fell several times, and when she couldn't get up, she'd push the alert button she wore around her neck. Police would break into a window to rescue her and take her to the hospital. In 2009, after yet another fall, she finally agreed to go into a nearby nursing home.

Doug and I were relieved that she was finally in a clean environment, free from clutter. She stayed there for several months until she died on December 25. Doug commented how ironic it was that his Jewish mother died on Christmas.

After her death, Doug had the unenviable task of going through his mom's clutter before most of it was hauled away in huge trash bins. In the mess, he found the key to his brother's safety deposit box which his mother had continued to pay for. Leslie had always bragged about how he had filled it with all kinds of material for future business ventures. When Doug finally opened it, he couldn't wait to get home to tell me what he'd found. "Guess what was inside of Leslie's safety deposit box?" he said smiling as he produced a tiny bent piece of steel, "Just one paper clip." After Leslie's troubled existence, we finally had something fun to remember him by.

CHAPTER 26

College Life

In 1980, our local newspaper wrote an article about me called, "The Write Stuff," a clever play off the movie title *The Right Stuff* about the Mercury Astronauts. I don't know how the newspaper found out about me, and I don't have a copy of the article, but I do remember it described the "amazing success story" of how I had managed to become editor of my high school newspaper despite my disability.

Emboldened by my success on the *Chimera Chronicle*, I applied to the journalism departments at a couple of colleges in New Jersey, the University of Maryland and Marquette University in Milwaukee, Wisconsin, where Aunt Jane had graduated with a degree in physical therapy.

I was accepted at all of them. I decided to cross Marquette off the list. Even though I loved the Mary Tyler Moore show set in a newsroom in Minneapolis, I hated winter weather and was afraid that if I went to Marquette, I'd end up working in bitterly cold Milwaukee after graduation. For someone born on

December 21, the first day of winter, it's amazing how much I detest cold weather.

I decided to stay in New Jersey and attend Seton Hall University in South Orange, about an hour and a half north of Willingboro. I loved its small campus and the beautiful 150-year-old Immaculate Conception Chapel in the center of the quad. I figured a smaller campus would be easier for me to navigate than some of the larger campuses I had visited. Seton Hall is a Catholic university founded in 1856 by Bishop James Roosevelt Bayley and named after his aunt, Saint Elizabeth Ann Seton. I figured Dad's parents would be thrilled that I had chosen a Catholic university.

Incoming freshmen were supposed to move into the dormitories the day after Labor Day, but Mom's husband John couldn't get that Tuesday off. So instead, Mom and John drove me to Seton Hall on Labor Day. When we arrived, the campus was mostly empty, except for a few upper-class resident assistants who received free room and board for overseeing the student dorms.

After helping me unpack, make my bed and settle in, Mom and John left, and I was all alone. There was nothing to do until the Student Government Welcome Back Mixer the following day, when my roommates were scheduled to arrive. I was anxious and scared and lonely. That night, I cried myself to sleep. The next day, I met my new roommates and pretended I had just arrived.

The Welcome Back Mixer was a revelation. Food and kegs of beer were set up on the quad. I couldn't believe that Seton Hall was welcoming us back with an unlimited supply of free beer. In 1980, the legal drinking age was 18, so I could drink all the alcohol I wanted.

During my first semester, I partied and drank to excess, especially at the campus pub, where I overindulged in 50-cent beers. When I got a D on my first college exam, I realized that I would flunk out if I didn't change my ways. I began to buckle down on my studies, and I limited my drinking to weekends. By the end of the semester, half the people I had partied with were gone or had already flunked out. When Mom and John came to visit, they stared in disbelief at all the empty beer and wine bottles I had proudly stacked on top of my desk.

CHAPTER 27

The Setonian

I IMMEDIATELY JOINED THE STAFF OF SETON Hall's weekly college newspaper, *The Setonian*. I was thrilled to be selected as a news reporter my freshman year. I don't remember much of what I wrote, but I do remember how excited I was when I saw my first college byline.

In the 1980s, we used word processors to type our stories, Exacto knives to cut out the columns of words printed by the typesetting machine, and rubber cement to paste the stories and headlines into place. Luckily, *Setonian* staffers had word processors at their disposal. In our journalism classrooms, we still used typewriters.

I became an assistant news editor the following year. I was assigned to cover some big stories, like the theft of our media center's video equipment, which made the front page in January 1982.

After working my way up the ranks as a reporter and editor, I was named the new Editor-in-Chief at the end of my junior year in May 1983.

CHAPTER 28

Living The Dream vs. Getting Paid

THE SUMMER BEFORE MY SENIOR YEAR, I WAS determined to work as an intern in New York City to get my foot in the door for a career in journalism. Some of my friends had already been offered jobs after completing internships at newspapers, magazines, TV or radio stations. I knew I could live on campus during the summer and take a bus into the city during the week.

In the spring of 1983, I had to choose between taking an unpaid summer internship at a TV station or a paid internship at Dun & Bradstreet's Technical Publishing Company in New York City.

Although I desperately wanted to take the internship at the TV station, I needed to make some money over the summer to pay for my books and expenses during the school year.

When classes ended in May, I reluctantly took the paid internship at Technical Publishing, which consisted of 20 trade and professional magazines. In high school, I had dreamed of working in TV or at a trendy magazine like *Time, Newsweek, Sports Illustrated*, or *Cosmopolitan*. At Technical Publishing, I was assigned to work at *World Construction* magazine, where I had the unglamorous task of writing short descriptions, called blurbs, about loaders and excavators. It was far cry from *Time* or *Cosmopolitan*.

But at least, in addition to getting paid, my internship would count toward the remaining credits I needed to graduate. My student loans were maxed out, and I was worried that my money would run out after the fall semester, leaving me one semester short of graduation. So I rolled the dice. I told my academic advisor that I wanted my summer internship to count as a full five-course semester worth 15 credits. Earning those credits in the summer would allow me to graduate after the fall semester ended in December.

On the last day of my summer internship, a publisher for several of the company's magazines, including the one I worked on, stopped by to tell me that he'd heard good things about me and wanted to hire me as an editorial assistant as soon as I graduated.

CHAPTER 29

Poor College Graduate

DURING MY LAST SEMESTER AT SETON HALL, ALL I wanted to do was enjoy my time as Editor-in-Chief of *The Setonian*, finish the few remaining credits I needed to graduate, and have as much fun as I could before leaving college in December. I didn't want to waste one precious minute of my dwindling college life looking for a job or going on interviews.

Since I had no other job prospects, I decided to take the job offer at Dun & Bradstreet. So instead of landing my dream job at *Time* or *Newsweek*, I started my career in technical publishing, a field that no journalism student dreams of entering.

Before I left Seton Hall, I put a deposit down on a small room for rent in a house not far from campus, within walking distance of the bus stop for New Jersey Transit, which ran daily buses into the city.

After celebrating the holidays back home in South Jersey, I called the publisher at Dun & Bradstreet to confirm my start date. When he answered the phone, he said, "I'm sorry, but the position I mentioned to you is no longer available." Stunned, I replied, "But you said I'd have a job waiting for me after I graduated." Luckily for me, Mom was in the kitchen listening to my side of the conversation. In the background she said forcefully, "Tell him you've already rented a place to live in North Jersey, and that you expect to start work next week. Tell him that if the position he promised you is no longer available, then he'll just have to find you something else."

I repeated her words verbatim. After an uncomfortable pause, the publisher said, "Well I guess I can find a job for you at one of my other magazines. When were you supposed to star…" Before he could complete the question, I blurted out, "Next Monday." "OK. I'll see you then," he said as he hung up the phone, unsure of what had just happened. Once again, Mom had saved the day.

That weekend, Mom and John drove me up to North Jersey, and I moved into my rented room. On Monday morning, I caught the bus and then took the subway to within walking distance of the huge, gleaming glass midtown building where Dun & Bradstreet's Technical Publishing Company was located.

When I went in to see the publisher, he told me I'd be working as an editorial assistant at *Fire Engineering*, a magazine I had never heard of. Before leaving, I said hesitantly, "Excuse me. What's the starting salary?" "$13,000," he replied without looking up.

CHAPTER 30

Rubber Cones

As I rode the elevator from the publisher's suite to the magazine's offices, I wondered, "What's *Fire Engineering*? What a weird name for a magazine. When I entered the lobby, I was greeted by a young, thin energetic woman with long black hair who would become a lifelong best friend. "Hi. I'm Linda McCauley," she smiled. "We're in here." I followed her back to a spacious office with two desks and lots of paper all over the place. She showed me to my desk which was easy to pick out. It was the clean one. She gave me a couple of recent issues to look through to familiarize myself with the magazine.

I learned that *Fire Engineering*, founded in 1877, covered training, education and management of emergency services personnel. I learned that a woman named Dorothy had just retired as managing editor after spending 45 years at the magazine. I couldn't imagine spending the next 45 years there.

Since Linda and I shared an office, we spent hours getting to know each other as we poured over page proofs and galleys of the monthly magazine.

One day Linda, who had been promoted to replace Dorothy as managing editor, asked me what my salary was since I had taken her old job. "$13,000," I admitted. "What! I can't believe that! When I was hired last year, I started at $11,000. I can't believe you're getting 13!"

Salary differences aside, we soon bonded over our mutual dislike of the magazine's new editor, a gruff, retired captain in the New York City fire department who had been hired because of his fire industry experience and contacts. Unfortunately, he had no editorial experience. He treated *Fire Engineering*'s female staff with open hostility. Once, when we tried to explain that we had to cut a paragraph from a column submitted by one of his firefighting buddies so that it would fit on the page, his Irish face reddened in anger, "Don't you dare edit my friend's words!" From that day on, we avoided bringing editorial changes to his attention whenever we could, in order to circumvent one of his sudden outbursts.

One day he snarled to me, "Your most important job is opening my mail." On another day, as he passed our office on the way to lunch, he looked in and sneered, "You both sit there all day doing nothing, like a couple of rubber cones."

When we weren't posing as rubber cones during the week, we would go out for happy hour or to the TKTS booth in Times Square to wait in line for discount tickets to Broadway shows, which we both loved. Some weekends, Linda took me to her home in Mount Vernon, where I met her parents Tom and Marianne McCauley. I especially loved Marianne, who went back to college to earn her bachelor's degree in the early 1970s, while juggling the needs of five young children.

When I talked to Marianne, she always took me seriously, which few of my other friend's mothers did. She punctuated our conversations with, "That's an interesting way of looking at things." Or, "Why do you feel that way?" Her empathy and capacity to listen to other points of view, even though they sometimes differed from her own, served her well during her tenure as Human Rights Commissioner for the city of Mount Vernon, New York.

Linda and I soon decided to rent the top floor of a house in Lodi, New Jersey, along with one of my former college roommates, Judy. There were only two bedrooms, and since Linda didn't know Judy and could pay more for a private room, I got stuck sharing a room, which meant that I had no privacy when Doug came to visit me during trips home on leave from the Army. We were still dating even though he was stationed in Germany.

Although I had finished my college classes in December, my commencement ceremony was in May 1984. A few weeks before the ceremony, I received a letter telling me that I had been selected to receive that year's Communication Achievement Award, given to the department's top senior. I also learned that I would be graduating cum laude, with honors, another unexpected surprise.

As I walked onto the stage, I couldn't revel in the moment or smile and wave to my family like the other graduates. I was too focused on keeping my balance in the low-heeled pointy black shoes Mom had bought me for the occasion. Every time I took a step, my ankles buckled and my heart raced in fear. "Don't fall. Don't fall," I repeated under my breath all the way to the stage and back. When I made it safely back to my seat without falling, I exhaled in gratitude.

That fall, Linda told me that she was leaving *Fire Engineering* to head the advertising department at a North Jersey real estate company. I didn't want to be a rubber cone without her, so a few weeks later, I left to take a job as a junior reporter and editor at small chain of weekly North Jersey newspapers, including the *Bergen News*.

CHAPTER 31

Momita

WHILE WORKING AT THE *BERGEN NEWS* IN November 1984, I saw a classified ad for a managing editor position at Ruspam Communications in Fort Lee, New Jersey, right across the George Washington Bridge from New York City. Since it wasn't far from where I lived in Lodi, I decided to go for an interview.

Ruspam published a bilingual magazine, *Sugar y Azucar*, that covered the worldwide sugar industry. When I arrived for my interview, I met the publisher, Richard Slimermeyer, who everyone called Dick, and Nilsa Galan-Pena who ran the financial side of the company.

After a brief interview, I was hired to fill the managing editor position. When my first issue was ready to go to the printer a few weeks later, I checked my name in the masthead. Under "Sheri Thomas" it said Assistant Editor. Furious, I marched into Dick Slimermeyer's office and demanded an explanation. "Well, we've never had a female managing editor, he said. "Well, you do now!" I replied angrily. I went back to my office, slammed the door and changed Assistant to Managing. Male chauvinism be damned!

At *Sugar y Azucar*, I was captivated by Nilsa's vibrancy and Puerto Rican heritage. She soon started inviting me to her house in Deer Park, Long Island for fun weekends spent drinking too much rum and coke, and salsa dancing with her family and friends. Nilsa, her husband David (a New York City policeman), her son Ivan, who would soon follow in his father's footsteps at the NYPD, and their daughter Frances, then 11, became my second family. I lovingly called Nilsa "Momita."

In retrospect, 1984 was a great year. In January, I met Linda at *Fire Engineering*. That summer, my sister Kim married handsome, blond Stephen Uhl, an electrical lineman who went on to manage the training of other linemen. (I adored him from the moment we met, and like I did with all the other males in the family, I bonded with him over our mutual love of sports.) In August, Carl Lewis, whom I had covered as sports editor of the *Chimera Chronicle*, equaled Jesse Owens' feat in the 1936 Olympics by winning gold medals in the 100 meters, 200 meters, 4x100 meter relay and the long jump at the Olympic Games in Los Angeles. And then in November, I met Momita.

CHAPTER 32

Honeymooners

IN BOOT CAMP, DOUG HAD BRIEFLY DATED A woman who became pregnant. They hastily got married and had a daughter named Randi. Doug wrote me with the news, which shocked me. Before I had a chance to write back, he called and told me the marriage was over.

After spending three years in Germany, Doug came back to the U.S. and was assigned to Fort Rucker, Alabama where he was presented with two strong incentives for reenlisting: a generous financial bonus and the opportunity to choose where he wanted to be stationed next. He picked Oahu, Hawaii where he worked at Wheeler Air Force Base as an Army air traffic controller. He spent his days off enjoying Hawaii's beautiful beaches, shopping for bargains at the International Market Place or trying traditional island dishes like poke and poi.

Doug invited me to spend Christmas with him in Hawaii in 1985. So I spent all year scrimping and saving for my airfare, while Doug scrimped and saved to give me the best time ever. The day before my 24th birthday on December 21, Doug met me with a big bouquet of flowers when I landed in Honolulu.

When we weren't sightseeing, Doug had only one thing on his mind. Round after round we went. After a few days, I woke up in excruciating pain and tried to pee. It was the sharpest pain I had ever felt. I didn't know what was wrong. "Doug, I think you should take me to the ER," I panted. As we waited to see a doctor, I thought, "Great. I finally made it to Hawaii, and now I'm sitting in the ER." Meanwhile, Doug was thinking, "What have I done to her?"

After listening to my symptoms, the doctor smiled and said, "In the old days, we called this honeymooner disease. I'll give you some medicine for the pain and some antibiotics to clear up your infection. And remember to urinate before and after sex." Doug was relieved that he hadn't permanently injured me. I was mortified.

CHAPTER 33

Philadelphia

THE ONLY PERSON OF ANY WEALTH IN OUR FAMILY was my mother's sister Roberta, who owned a successful advertising agency in Philadelphia with her husband, Robert Shimer. Founded in the 1970s, Shimer von-Cantz, combined Robert's last name with her maiden name of Cantz. She added "von" to give it panache.

They lived in big houses, and Aunt Roberta even had a chauffeur to drive her back and forth to the agency. They also owned a yacht called *Promises Kept* complete with a private chef. In the 1980s, my best friend Linda and I enjoyed an evening aboard, our every whim catered to.

Aunt Roberta was eccentric, and I adored her, but I hated the way she chain-drank vodka, one after the other, on a daily basis. It reminded me of my alcoholic father.

At a family gathering in 1988, Aunt Roberta pulled me aside and said, "You should come work at the agency." After four years in the dull world of technical publishing, I was ready for a change, so I accepted her offer on the spot.

My friend Linda was ready for a career change too, and she jumped at the chance to move to Philadelphia with me. We even found an apartment complex in town, complete with a pool and a gym. I got Linda an interview with the creative director at Shimer, and we were sure she'd be hired as well. Her portfolio was full of ads she had written for the real estate company she now worked for in North Jersey. But as the creative director scanned her portfolio, she asked, "You can write about real estate, but can you sell toothpaste?" Linda left dumbfounded, shocked that she wasn't offered a job on the spot.

Over the next few days, Linda interviewed at a couple of other agencies, but got basically the same response; creative directors wanted someone who had experience selling products not real estate. With no job prospects in Philadelphia, Linda returned to her job in North Jersey, leaving me to live on my own for the first time.

I soon found a charming studio apartment in an historic building in the Society Hill section of the city near Independence Mall and just a short cobblestoned walk from Shimer vonCantz. I loved the old cobblestoned sidewalks, except on rainy or snowy days when they became slick and slippery, especially dangerous for someone like me.

Even though I missed Linda and Nilsa, I was looking forward to having my own place so that when Doug visited, we would finally have some privacy.

CHAPTER 34

Shimer vonCantz

ON MY FIRST DAY AT SHIMER VONCANTZ, I WAS told I'd be the assistant traffic manager. I had no idea what that entailed, but I reported to the traffic manager, a young vibrant woman named Debbie. She explained that we were responsible for keeping track of the progress of each ad the agency produced, from start to finish. All day long, I was running paperwork from office to office. By the time I got home, my feet were painfully swollen.

For the next 14 months, I literally worked my ass off. I lost so much weight running around the agency, that my clothes barely stayed on.

Besides the physical stress I was putting on my body, my creative side was suffering as well. I decided I wanted to be a copywriter. Every time I saw our creative director, Karen Grace, I told her that I would be willing to try copywriting on my own time so that it wouldn't interfere with my traffic department duties.

Karen finally agreed to give me a small job for one of the agency's pro bono accounts, the Ronald

McDonald House. I wrote their holiday newsletter, which I named *Happy McHolidays*. It wasn't copywriting, but at least it proved I could write, and Karen started throwing some copywriting jobs my way.

I wrote a few pro bono ads for a local education association urging kids to stay in school. My first ad headline was, "Here are 200,000 Reasons to Stay in School." The copy begins with, "Studies show that if you graduate from high school, you can expect to earn $200,000 *more* during your lifetime than a high school dropout." The second ad was headlined, "If You Think School Is Boring, Try One Of These Exciting Jobs." I got a newspaper and cut out lots of classified ads for unappealing jobs like janitor, dishwasher, parking lot attendant etc., and gave them to the art director who scattered them all around the headline.

One of my ads even won an award from the Graphic Arts Association in a contest they were running to promote print advertising. "Try Zapping this ad," featured a picture of a VCR remote control. The copy begins, "You can't, can you? You can turn the page, but this print ad won't disappear. It will still be there the next time you pick up this publication."

But still, I never made it out of the traffic department. Another dream thwarted.

CHAPTER 35

Worth The Wait

WHILE I WAS WORKING AT SHIMER VONCANTZ, Doug was newly stationed at Fort Belvoir, Virginia to manage air traffic control operations at the Pentagon heliport in D.C. In January 1989, he told me he was ready to leave the Army. I was relieved, because I knew I wouldn't be a good Army wife, dutifully moving with Doug to wherever he got stationed.

I had moved too much as a kid, and I hated it. I wanted to get married, put down roots and never move again. So much for wishes. Doug and I have moved 10 times since we've been married.

I helped Doug put together his resume. He wanted to stay in aviation, but he had been diagnosed with caracatonis, and his vision was getting worse. He was concerned it would hinder his ability as an air traffic controller. Besides that, it was a high-pressure job. Doug decided to look for a job in air traffic system management and work with the FAA to update its navigation systems.

In May 1989, just four months after leaving the Army, he was offered a position as an aviation system analyst with a small private company called MiTech. He would be part of a team working with the FAA to develop air traffic management systems. His starting salary was $30,000. *Wow! $30,000!* We couldn't believe it. To us, it sounded like a small fortune since it was double our present salaries. I told Doug we could start planning our wedding.

Mom, born during the Depression, had taught me to be frugal, which was good, since we'd be paying for our own wedding. We found a catering hall in South Jersey that only charged $23 a head, and we booked our wedding and reception for Sunday, October 22, 1989, with 75 guests. We shopped around for the cheapest prices for the florist, DJ and photographer, and we asked Doug's best friend Bill Fox to videotape the wedding.

It was the '80s so I had big hair and a big dress with puffy sleeves. Since I couldn't wear heels, Mom decorated a pair of white satin ballerina slippers with lace and pearls. The bridesmaids wore forest green gowns, with puffy sleeves, of course.

We had a small wedding party. Linda was matron of honor, and her then husband Michael was Doug's best man, since Bill would be busy videotaping. My sister Kim and her husband Steve were joined in the wedding party by my brother Mark and his wife Joan who flew up from Florida.

Before his marriage in 1985, Mark sometimes drank too much, just as I was prone to do. Joan had threatened to leave him unless he stopped drinking. He went to Alcoholics Anonymous and has been sober ever since. Mark doesn't like to take credit for turning his life around, but I'm so proud of him. Mark and Joan still live in Naples, not far from their 27-year-old son Jacob.

Steve almost backed out of attending the wedding when he realized that we were getting married during the Eagles-Cowboys game. Since Kim wouldn't let him skip our big day to watch the game, he put a small transistor radio inside his tuxedo jacket and listened to the game during the ceremony through a small earpiece.

Doug and I finally got married on October 22, 1989. (left to right) my brother-in-law Steve, my sister Kim (seated), Doug's best man Michael, me, Doug, my matron-of-honor Linda, my sister-in-law Joan (seated) and my brother Mark.

CHAPTER 36

Welcome To Tiny Living

FIVE MONTHS BEFORE OUR WEDDING, DOUG started his new job at MiTech in Washington D.C. My career had stalled at Shimer vonCantz, so I gave my notice, cleaned out my studio apartment in Philadelphia and got ready to move south.

I asked Doug to find us a one-bedroom furnished apartment. A few days before the wedding, Doug called to tell me that he had found the perfect one-bedroom apartment for us in Silver Spring, Maryland in a building with a beautiful lobby, within walking distance of the Metro, which Doug took to work. I told him that it sounded perfect.

Dad offered to pay for our honeymoon. I found out later that his new wife had actually paid for it, which didn't surprise me. Doug and I had a great honeymoon in the Cayman Islands, and I made sure to pee before and after sex so I wouldn't get another painful bout of honeymooner disease.

As soon as our flight landed back in D.C., Doug drove us straight to our new apartment. We held hands as we walked into the lobby. Doug was right.

The lobby was beautiful. It was ornately decorated with large framed paintings and featured the biggest chandelier I had ever seen. So far, so good. "I could get used to living here," I gushed. "With a lobby this beautiful, I can't wait to see our apartment."

We took the elevator up to the fourth floor, and Doug proudly opened the door. Then he surprised me by swooping me up and carrying me over the threshold into our new apartment. I was all smiles until he put me down.

As I looked around, I was devastated. "This isn't a one-bedroom apartment," I screeched at Doug. "Yes, it is," he said. "This is one room, just like you wanted." Clearly, I hadn't explained to him that a one-bedroom apartment was one bedroom *plus* a separate kitchen/living room area.

The tiny studio had a small bathroom and a kitchen area with a sink and a stainless-steel counter with two burners underneath that you could pull out to cook on and then push back in after dinner and a college-dorm-size refrigerator. There was only one closet, not big enough to fit my clothes, much less Doug's.

"Where's the bed?" I asked. "Right here," said Doug as he pulled down a Murphy bed mounted to the wall. Its old bedframe squeaked so loudly whenever we had sex, the old ladies living below complained about us almost every day.

CHAPTER 37

Full Circle

ONCE THE SHOCK OF STUDIO LIVING WORE OFF, I started looking for a job. To make some money in the meantime, I started working at a temp agency doing word processing or data entry. The work was boring, but it was interesting to see so many different companies.

One day, I saw an ad for a public relations/newsletter editor for an organization in Washington, D.C. I called and scheduled an interview. When I got there, I saw the name on the office door: American Association on Mental Retardation. After the interview, I was hired.

I took the job, not realizing at the time that I had come full circle: from being diagnosed as "mentally retarded" to working in the field of "mental retardation."

PART FOUR:

Knock Knock

CHAPTER 38

Water Never Tasted So Good

I wasn't thrilled about working for the American Association on Mental Retardation, and so every morning, I perused the want ads. One day in November 1990, a small ad caught my eye: "MARKETING, Unlimited earning potential. Call Kerry Reid at ..."

Unlimited earning potential sounded good to me, so I dialed the number. When Kerry Reid picked up the phone, he changed my life forever. Over the next seven years, Kerry not only taught me about sales, but he also taught me valuable life lessons that have guided me ever since. He taught me about persistence and how to master my emotions to get the most out of every day. Not only did he become my mentor, but Kerry and his wife Patty and their daughters, Heather and Logan, became dear friends.

That November day when I heard his warm, folksy voice for the first time, he explained that he represented a company called National Safety

Associates, or NSA, that sold water filters that made water taste better.

Later, at our interview, he pulled out the company's smallest filter, the 10 P, (p for portable) with two parts that unscrewed like a thermos. He poured water through the part that had the activated carbon filter into the second part that was a cup for drinking and then handed the cup to me. As soon as I tasted the water, I could tell the difference. It didn't have the chemical aftertaste of tap water. I was amazed. It was the most effective sales presentation I had ever seen. Kerry simply let the product sell itself.

I couldn't wait to get my own 10 P or countertop unit and start drinking all the pure filtered water my bladder could hold.

Today, people are accustomed to drinking filtered or bottled water. But in the early 1990s, you had to introduce people to the idea that their tap water tasted so bad that they needed to buy a water filter to make it taste better.

Kerry couldn't wait to show me how much money I could make by selling water filters myself or by getting other people to sell them for me, which was the easiest way to make even more money.

It was my first introduction to multi-level marketing. At NSA, sales associates bought water filters from the company at wholesale and then sold them to customers at a higher retail price, pocketing the difference. Many companies operate this way, including Amway and Mary Kay, which Mom tried her hand at without success.

Kerry explained NSA's various commission levels by drawing steps on a white board. He said that most people started at the second level as a director by purchasing $5,000 worth of filters, a mix of the portable, countertop and under-the-sink models.

I had never heard of a job where you paid money to make money, but Kerry made it sound so easy. I signed up immediately. I didn't know where I'd get $5,000, but I knew that if I could just pour water through a 10 P in front of enough people, that I'd have no problem selling my inventory or recruiting lots of other people to work underneath me. I dreamed I'd be making thousands of dollars a month. Spending $5,000 to get started sounded like a real bargain.

I couldn't wait to tell Doug how much money I could make if we could just scrape $5,000 together. I was so excited that Doug agreed I should give it a try. He said we could borrow the money from our credit cards. Soon, boxes and boxes of water filters arrived at our door.

Over the next year and a half, I did manage to sell some water filters and recruit some people, but I never made the thousands of dollars a month that Kerry had initially described.

CHAPTER 39

Door-To-Door

In April 1992, I learned that Kerry had started another company. Curious, I asked him about it. "It's called Dominion Business Promotions, and we promote service stations like Exxon and Mobil by selling cards door-to-door that offer customers free services, like oil changes and tire rotations, and discounts on car repairs. Here, I'll show you."

Always ready with a sales presentation, Kerry opened his desk drawer and took out a 5x7 red and blue card with lots of squares on the top and bottom, tucked inside of a clear plastic sleeve.

He knocked on the desk, five times, followed by a pause, then two more quick knocks. As he handed me the card, he smiled and began, "Hi, I'm Kerry from Backlick Mobil on Backlick Road…" Then he went on to explain the savings the service station was offering to new customers.

It was the same 30-second presentation I would learn to say, and then teach others to say, thousands of times over the next five years. In the process, I would finally make the thousands and thousands of dollars that I thought I would make selling water filters.

The only thing that changed from contract to contract was the name and location of the service station. We promoted every brand of gas station, from Mobil, to Shell, to Exxon. Dominion Business Promotions (DBP), which Kerry and his wife Patty started in their townhouse in Springfield, Virginia, grew to hundreds of salespeople in over ten cities across the country.

DBP initially promoted gas stations that had service bays, but as the company grew, we also promoted dry cleaners and pizza chains like Domino's, using the same basic door-to-door presentation, modified only slightly to fit the business.

It was the perfect business for the early 1990s. People were still receptive to opening their doors to strangers, and they loved all the free services they could get from a business right in their neighborhood. We sold an inexpensive product that everyone could afford, and we earned high commissions on each $36 sale, up to $20 per card.

CHAPTER 40

I Am Woman

I was the only saleswoman in the company, and I was determined to outsell every man at DBP. And in the beginning, I did. I outsold all the men during DBP's first monthly sales contest. I consistently sold over 50 cards a week, over 200 that month. They couldn't believe that a woman limping from house to house, who could only reach half as many houses as they did, actually beat them. Even though I knocked on fewer doors, I made more sales than they did because I worked harder at every door, doggedly answering every objection until the customer gave in and went to get their checkbook.

We sold cards every day in all weather, no matter how cold or hot it was or whether it was raining or snowing. The worse the weather was, the more cards we sold, because more people were home.

A positive mental attitude, perseverance, and the ability to control your emotions were, according to Kerry, just as important as learning the presentation and objections.

Kerry motivated us using his favorite books and stories and taught us how to motivate our own sales teams. After reading hundreds of motivational books, Kerry had narrowed them down to a few favorites, which he ordered in bulk from the publishers and gave out to everyone he hired.

Every Saturday at 10 a.m., the team leaders and salespeople gathered in the office for pep talks by Kerry. Afterwards, we got our new territory and headed out to begin knocking on doors.

The first book Kerry gave me in July 1992 was *The Greatest Salesman in the World* by Og Mandino. I still have it, its cover dented with teeth marks from our yellow labrador, Precious, who loved to snatch the little book from my hands to get my attention. That teeth-marked book is my most prized possession. Here are some of my favorite excerpts that have helped shape my life:

> "I will greet this day with love in my heart. I will laud my enemies and they will become friends; I will encourage my friends and they will become brothers. Always will I dig for reasons to applaud; never will I scratch for excuses to gossip." In these divisive times, I wish more people could find reasons to applaud rather than criticize each other.

> *"I will persist until I succeed."* Kerry told us that if we persisted and kept knocking on doors, we would succeed. He related this to Thomas Edison who made 1,000 unsuccessful attempts to invent the light bulb before he finally succeeded.
>
> *"I am nature's greatest miracle.* Since the beginning of time never has there been another with my mind, my heart, my eyes, my ears, my hands, my hair, my mouth. None that came before me, none that live today, and none that come tomorrow can walk and talk and move and think exactly like me…"

Kerry's words of wisdom and *The Greatest Salesman in the World* catapulted a young woman with cerebral palsy and no sales experience to even greater heights at Dominion Business Promotions.

My mentor, Kerry Reid, who started Dominion Business Promotions (DBP) in 1992, changed my life forever.

CHAPTER 41

To Richmond And Beyond

KERRY DEVELOPED HIS BEST SALESPEOPLE INTO team leaders who would manage their own sales teams. Team leaders still sold cards, but they also got a commission on cards their team sold. Jeff Bishop and I were the first team leaders. Then, the best team leaders were promoted to district managers, responsible for hiring and training new salespeople in one of the cities DBP was expanding into. Once you were successful as a district manager, you could become a regional manager.

Kerry opened the first district office in Baltimore. A few months later, Kerry asked me to move to Richmond as the company's second district manager. Since I would now be earning more than enough to support us, Doug took a hiatus from his career in D.C. and moved with me to Richmond.

Everyone who worked for Kerry was an independent contractor. Before I moved to Richmond, I formed a corporation for tax purposes. I called my company Knox Unlimited, which rhymed with knocks, to remind me of the thousands of doors I knocked on during my years with Kerry.

After DBP opened offices in Virginia Beach and Raleigh, North Carolina, I was promoted to regional manager to oversee those cities while I continued to run Richmond.

When Atlanta's district manager left the company in 1995, I jumped at the chance to relocate there since I had fond childhood memories of Georgia, happily playing with my dog Snoopy. As a regional manager in Atlanta, I ran that office while still supervising sales activities in Richmond, Raleigh and Virginia Beach.

After 11 months in Atlanta, Doug was anxious to get back to his own career in aviation systems management. A few weeks later, Jeff Bishop left the company, and Kerry needed someone to run the Baltimore office, located in Reisterstown, Maryland. I immediately told Kerry that I was willing to move to Maryland to run that office so that Doug could resume his career in D.C.

As I wrapped up things in Atlanta, Doug contacted a real estate agent in Maryland. She found us a townhouse for rent in Columbia, halfway between D.C. and Baltimore. This time, I approved it via photographs before making the move. I didn't want to repeat our first one-bedroom/studio mishap.

Doug drove one car with our dog, Precious, and I drove the other. We arrived in Maryland on January

6, 1996 to meet the moving van in Columbia. The next day, a major blizzard blanketed the area in over two feet of snow.

Columbia, a planned community in Howard County, Maryland, turned out to be the perfect location for us, with Baltimore to the north and Washington, D.C. to the south. Doug drove down I-95 South to the Metro station for work, and I drove a half hour north to the office in Reisterstown.

In 1995, Kerry sent me a handwritten note which I framed, "Congratulations on your great week and being top district. There was never a doubt in my mind of your success. Your determination and work ethic guarantees it. You deserve all your success."

PART FIVE:

My True Self

CHAPTER 42

Changing The Channel

UNTIL THE AGE OF 36, I WAS ABLE TO WALK VIGorously with what some people called a slight limp and others described as an imbalanced and pronounced gait. No matter how I walked, nothing slowed me down.

Five years of walking countless miles to knock on countless doors, however, finally caught up to me. By July 1997, my feet couldn't take it anymore. Every time I took a step, my left foot recoiled in pain and my ankle buckled, causing me to lose my balance. After consulting with a foot and ankle orthopedist in Baltimore, I realized that I could no longer walk door-to-door. My days at Dominion Business Promotions were over.

I went into a months-long funk. To pull myself out of it, I started to reread some of my favorite motivational books. One day, I found a small maroon paperback book hidden behind some other books in my bookcase. When Kerry had given it to me years before, I had barely looked at it. Now, its strange title, *Psycho-Pictography*, intrigued me, and I began to read it.

Written by Vernon Howard in 1965, the book used mental pictures, as he called them, to convey ideas and psychological concepts. The mental pictures were entertaining and easy to remember.

One of my favorites is called, *How to Avoid the Horror Films in Your Everyday Life*. "Suppose you slip out of bed some morning with the resolve to make it a cheery day. You determine to think and do nothing but bright and constructive things. Then you walk to the television set and turn it on—to a horror film. You sit down to watch mad monsters tear up the earth. You see nothing but vicious destruction." ... Millions of people "start their day with their own horror film. And it is an endless performance; it runs deep into the night. That horror film is in the mind. We call it negative imagination."

I learned that how we're feeling is directly connected to what our mind is focused on. If we don't like the thoughts running through our mind, we have the power to think about something else. We can change our thoughts just like we can change the TV channel; we can turn off the horror movie and find a comedy instead.

During my later bipolar episodes, I was not mentally healthy, and it was impossible to control my mind no matter how much I wanted to. Without medication, my brain short-circuited like the faulty circuit breaker that caused our house lights to flicker on and off before it was repaired.

CHAPTER 43

True Calling

AFTER READING *PSYCHO-PICTOGRAPHY*, I REALized that I had spent the last five years measuring my self-esteem by the number of sales I made.

Now, I was determined to rediscover my true self. As I began this new chapter in my life, I found myself longing for spirituality. Although I had been raised Catholic, I stopped going to church as a teenager. I felt the Catholic Church was too confining for me. Doug had been raised Jewish, but when he was in the Army, he gravitated toward Christianity.

In early 1999, I told Doug that I wanted to find a local non-denominational church for us to attend so that we could embrace spirituality and make some new friends.

The problem was that I had no idea of what kind of non-denominational church I was looking for. All I knew was that I wanted to find a church that accepted everyone.

One Sunday, I spotted a small ad in the newspaper for a nearby church that said, "Everyone was welcome." I wrote down the information and told Doug that we should check out a service the following weekend.

The church was located in a brick building right behind the same shopping center that we went to every week. We had seen the building before, but we thought it was a day care center since it had a playground out front. We had no idea that it was actually an interfaith center, common in Columbia, which was shared by two different congregations, Christ United Methodist Church and the one we wanted to try out, the Unitarian Universalist Congregation of Columbia (UUCC). I had no idea what Unitarian Universalism was, but I wanted to find out.

When we walked in the door the following Sunday, we were greeted warmly by Ruth Smith who gave each of us a hug. As we sat down and listened to the service, Doug and I were immediately drawn to the seven guiding principles of Unitarian Universalism, which include: promoting the inherent worth and dignity of every person, justice, equity and compassion in human relations and respect for the interdependent web of all existence of which we are a part.

After being diagnosed as "mentally retarded" as a toddler and facing so much discrimination throughout my life because of my disability, how could I not love a religion that believes in promoting the inherent worth and dignity of every person?

I'm proud that we are a liberal religion that embraces everyone, regardless of race, creed, disability, or sexual orientation. We have fought for social justice, civil rights and marriage equality, but we must work harder to recognize and fight discrimination, oppression and racial injustice.

As my spirituality deepened, I began to look for ways to promote the inherent worth and dignity of every person, especially those with disabilities. I was finally ready to embrace my true calling.

CHAPTER 44

Disability Advocate

THE ANNUAL CHURCH AUCTION, WHICH I LATER chaired in 2006, raised a lot of money for UUCC. Attendees bid on member-donated products, services, events or dinners. Doug and I were invited to attend an outdoor murder-mystery party on a warm summer Saturday night hosted by Andrea and John Holt, who had also recently joined UUCC. Marni McNeese, another new UUCC member, was also given a free ticket to attend. That night marked the beginning of life-long friendships with Andrea, John, and Marni.

I found out that Marni worked for Howard County Government in Disability Services, helping residents access services, programs, and resources for citizens with disabilities. She also worked with her boss, Joyce Lehrer, to staff the county's Commission on Disabilities. That immediately piqued my interest, since I was looking for ways to help people with disabilities.

The other reason we bonded so quickly was that we both loved sports. She was the first woman

I had ever met who was as crazy about sports as I was, and she soon started taking me to Maryland women's basketball games in College Park. Marni made sure that we had accessible seating right on the court so I wouldn't have to navigate stairs. We joined the Rebounders, the team's fan club and traveled with them to games and tournaments, including the NCAA Final Four tournament in Boston where we saw the Terrapins win their first national championship in 2006.

Every January, the church's religious education teachers took a month-long break from teaching their regular Sunday morning classes, and UUCC asked for a volunteer who would be willing to teach the children about a special topic. On the last Sunday in January, the service would cover the same topic.

I told our religious education director that I wanted to teach the kids about disability awareness during the month of January in 2000. I asked Marni to help me because she loved kids and worked in the disability field.

Marni was great. She found children's books on disability awareness, and we developed fun things to do with the kids, like showing them what braille looked like, letting them try out crutches, and turning the sound off on the TV to show what it is like to see without hearing and why closed-captioning is so important.

On the last Sunday in January, the kids joined the rest of the congregation in the sanctuary for the disability awareness service featuring many of the things we had taught the children.

We stressed the importance of using the proper language to identify people with disabilities: We had the congregation repeat after us: "Sheri has a disability" instead of "Sheri is handicapped, crippled or disabled." "Bob has an intellectual disability" instead of "Bob is mentally retarded." "Mary has a mental health condition" instead of "Mary is mentally ill."

Today, according to the National Center on Disability and Journalism (www.ncdj.org) it is preferrable to ask the person how they would like to be described and use the actual name of the disability, if possible, as long as the diagnosis has come from a reputable source, such as a medical professional or other licensed professional. Today, if it's relevant to a conversation or situation, I'll say, "I have cerebral palsy." I'm not "afflicted with" or "suffering from" cerebral palsy. If I'm just talking about sports, the fact that I have cerebral palsy is irrelevant.

On the 30th anniversary of the signing of the ADA (July 26, 2020), I co-lead another church service about disability awareness with Marian Vessels, a member of Channing Memorial Church, Unitarian Universalist, where Doug and I are also members.

After the service we did together in January 2000, Marni encouraged me to apply to fill an opening on the Howard County Commission on Disabilities. After the positive reviews I received from the congregation, I was ready to do more.

In the cover letter I wrote to County Executive Jim Robey, I explained why I wanted to fill the vacancy on the commission. "In 1997, I reluctantly gave up my (sales) business. My cerebral palsy and years of physical pounding finally took their toll, and I turned my attention from business success to humanitarian and social justice issues—including disability awareness advocacy. In January, I developed a disability awareness special curriculum for my church. I have a passion for inclusion and equality. I lead by example… I look forward to hearing from you and serving the county in the future." A few weeks later, the county council passed a resolution appointing me to the commission, where I served for 10 years, eventually becoming its chairperson.

While serving on the commission's access committee, I worked with Harriet Fisher and met her amazing son Jason, who has severe cerebral palsy that affects his entire body and speech. He is in a wheelchair, needs assistance, and his speech is hard for others to understand. Yet Jason persevered with the support and dedication of his parents, Harriet and John, to graduate not only from high school, but from college and law school as well. Harriet became a tireless advocate for her son and others, and today, Jason is a lawyer, married and living in Richmond, Virginia.

In 2002, my doctor advised me to start using a cane for both support and balance. At first, I resisted the idea, but as I learned how to use a cane, I realized it made walking a little easier. A few years ago, I bought a walker with a seat attached so that I can sit and rest if I get tired during longer outings. For short walks, I can still get by with just a cane. My hands work fine, although spasticity in my fingers, and now arthritis, makes it hard for me to write or do fine motor skills like opening bottles or bags of chips.

It's hard for someone without a disability to understand how frustrating it is for someone using a scooter or wheelchair who can't use the sidewalk because there are no curb cuts, for example, or can't use the bathroom because it isn't accessible, or can't get on the train because the elevator to the platform is out of order.

My friend, Linda, discovered this when we spent a week together in Newport, Rhode Island, much of which was built before the ADA. When we went on a walking tour of the town, I was using a scooter and many of the sidewalks had no curb cuts, so I was unable to get off the sidewalk and the tour left without us. Linda was also shocked at how many people stepped directly in front of me during house tours, as if I wasn't even there. That week opened her eyes to just a few of the accessibility issues people with disabilities face on a daily basis.

On the disabilities commission, I urged our county executive to make the meeting room in our county government building accessible. When you entered the large chamber, you looked down to a pit at the bottom where the county council was seated on a dais. The only way to join the meeting was to walk down several steep steps.

On the night we submitted our proposal to the county council, the commission agreed that I'd be the best person to demonstrate how inaccessible the chamber was.

Marni, who came with me, said, "Work it, girl!" When my name was called, I began an extraordinarily slow, painful descent, with my cane loudly punctuating each step. By the time I got to the bottom of the pit to give my testimony, the council members realized they had no choice but to approve funding for the renovation.

Taking a business-minded approach, I often would point out that our committee saved the county money because it was cheaper for us to suggest accessibility changes that could be incorporated *before* construction, rather than have the county spend even more money once a building had been completed.

AMC Movie Theatres executives flew in from Kansas to meet with our Access Committee to find out what accessibility features should be incorporated into all the new theatres they were building, including one in Columbia. We requested more room between the seat rows so that you didn't have to get up when people walked in front of you, handrails, better lighting, large accessible bathrooms, and more seats designated for people with disabilities, including ones with a space next them for a wheelchair or scooter. I am proud to say that they incorporated our suggestions, which still thrills me whenever I visit our local AMC Theatre.

Marni and I at a Maryland women's basketball team event in the early 2000s with Head Coach Brenda Frese.

CHAPTER 45

Taking Advocacy To A Whole New Level

I AGREED TO REPRESENT THE HOWARD COUNTY Commission on Disabilities on a new statewide organization called the Maryland Alliance of Disability Commissions and Committees. Alliance members met once a month in the same conference room where our county commission meetings were held, making it convenient for me to attend their meetings.

The Alliance was formed so members of disability commissions throughout Maryland could share ideas and information. We also wanted to have a voice in state and national legislation.

During one of the Alliance meetings, we found out that Baltimore City was working with the Motor Vehicle Administration (MVA) and its police department to catch people illegally using handicapped parking spaces (or accessible parking spaces as we advocates call them). Often, non-disabled family members or acquaintances think they are entitled to park in these spaces even though the person for whom the plates or placards were issued is not with them. That's illegal.

Montgomery County's disability commission also did groundbreaking work to pass legislation for universal design and to increase employment opportunities for people with disabilities that other Alliance members then introduced in their own counties.

In 2004, The Maryland Alliance of Disability Commissions and Committees supported legislation to create a state cabinet-level Department of Disabilities.

Nationally, Alliance members helped to pass the Mathew Shepard and James Byrd Hate Crimes Prevention Act of 2009 which expanded the federal hate crime law to include crimes motivated by a victim's disability, in addition to race, actual or perceived gender, sexual orientation, or gender identity.

The Alliance also worked to pass Rosa's Law, introduced by Maryland Senator Barbra Mikulski in 2009, which changed references to "mental retardation" in federal legislation to "intellectual disability." The law was named after a Maryland girl, Rosa Marcellino, who has Down Syndrome. As someone who has been hurt by the words "mentally retarded," I was thrilled to see Rosa's Law signed into law by President Barack Obama.

In 2005, I was honored by the commission with its Individual Achievement Award. In a letter, Maryland Delegate Gail Bates of Howard County wrote, "We are fortunate to have someone like you, who worked tirelessly to render the Banneker Room of the George Howard Building accessible to all our citizens. In addition, your efforts to obtain closed captioning on GTV (local government TV) and your continuous service on the state level as Vice-Chairperson of the Maryland Alliance (of Disability Commissions and Committees) help make Maryland and Howard County so wonderful."

PART SIX:

On Top of Everything

CHAPTER 46

Three Weeks

BESIDES MY HUSBAND, THE TWO MEN I SPENT the most time with were my sister Kim's husband, Steve Uhl, and my mentor Kerry Reid.

After living for many years in northern Virginia, Kerry and his wife Patty and their two daughters, Heather and Logan, settled in Delaware, just outside of Rehoboth Beach. Kerry soon turned his attention to another business opportunity, Pre-Paid Legal (now called Legal Shield), which offers legal services and credit monitoring via multi-level marketing to its members for a low monthly fee. Kerry found immediate success and rose to a lucrative executive level with the company.

In the early 2000s, Kerry was diagnosed with throat cancer and underwent months of chemo and radiation. For over a year, he could only drink Ensure. Then he underwent an operation at Johns Hopkins in Baltimore that opened up his throat so he could eat again. Kerry regained his strength, and we all thought he had beaten cancer. Months later, however, it came back more virulent than ever, and his condition became terminal.

Kerry loved boxing, and he used to host parties at his house so that we could all gather to watch the big pay-for-view fights. The night we watched George Foreman knock out Michael Moorer to regain the heavyweight title at the age of 45 was unforgettable. Kerry made one final trip to Maryland to take me to my first live boxing match. He died on March 30, 2006 at the age of 55.

Steve started his career as a lineman, climbing dangerously high on telephone poles to fix downed power lines. He then moved into management, coordinating training of linemen throughout the northeast. Kim and Steve lived in Boyertown, Pennsylvania, with their two children, Alicia and Chris.

Steve was diagnosed with terminal lung cancer in 2005. After returning home from a visit with his ailing mother, he complained of head pain. His doctor said it was a sinus infection. When antibiotics didn't relieve his pain after a few weeks, doctors ordered a PET scan. After reviewing the scan, doctors decided to perform diagnostic surgery. During the surgery, I anxiously waited with Kim in the hospital's lobby. Afterward, his surgeon confirmed our worst fears. Cancer had metastasized from his lungs to his brain, which was why his head had been hurting so much. He was given no more than a year to live.

My world turned upside down. I wanted to be with Kim, Steve and the kids as much as possible. Although he was accepted into a clinical trial, it didn't work. The only blessing was that once Steve quit the clinical trial, his appetite returned, and he rallied for a few precious months to celebrate Thanksgiving and Christmas. In early 2006, his body and strength diminished. In April, hospice care set up a hospital bed at home, in the sunroom he had built.

I rushed to Pennsylvania. For the first three days, hospice provided 24-hour care. On day four, no one from hospice arrived. Surprised, I called to ask why. I was told Steve's insurance only covered three days of full hospice care and that, going forward, they would only come two or three times a week to bathe him and refill his medication. I demanded a meeting with the hospice manager.

When she arrived the following morning and sat across from me in the sunroom, I told her that even if I had to pay for nurses out of my own pocket, I expected Steve to get the 24-hour hospice care he was entitled to. With that, her demeanor softened, and she offered to review Steve's insurance coverage herself. Later that afternoon, she called to tell me that she had personally authorized 24-hour hospice care to resume immediately.

On the day after Easter, April 17, 2006, Steve took his last breath as I stood at his bedside. He was just 48.

Two of the best men in my life had died within three weeks of each other.

CHAPTER 47

Frank-N-Steins

BY 2006, DAD, TIRED OF ROAMING THE COUNTRY selling RV campground memberships, had settled in Texas and opened a small hot dog restaurant called *Frank-N-Steins Grill* with his last wife Sandra.

As an adult, I had little contact with my father. I would call him around Christmas, and we'd spend a few awkward moments talking about football before he hurriedly hung up the phone. Every time I thought about him, painful childhood memories bubbled to the surface.

I hadn't seen him in years, but in 2008, I had a change of heart. With Dad now in his 70s, I realized that in order to move forward, it was time to make peace with him. I called my sister Kim and told her that we were going to Texas.

Dad was thrilled when I called to tell him we were planning to come see him. When we landed in Austin a few weeks later, we followed our rental car's GPS to a little trailer in the country where Dad lived with Sandra and his two dogs. We spent the next day at *Frank-N-Steins* sampling the menu and helping out where we could. Dad took us to each table and proudly introduced us to his customers. Kim and I were shocked at how much he'd aged. We ended up having a great trip. The weight of my childhood suddenly felt lighter.

Doug and I spent that Christmas with Kim in Pennsylvania. The next evening, we went to a movie. When we got back in the car, Kim had several frantic messages from Sandra saying that Dad had been rushed to the hospital. He had emergency surgery to repair his ruptured colon. Even though he recovered, he was diagnosed with terminal cancer several months later. I flew out to Texas with Kim and my brother Mark to see Dad one last time. He died on August 2, 2010 at the age of 73.

Visiting Dad in Texas in 2008.

CHAPTER 48

Brain Pain

MY HEADACHES INTENSIFIED IN BOTH SEVERITY and duration. I always carried sinus medicine with me in a little pill case. My family and friends always saw me popping pills, which I could swallow even without water. Debilitated by the pain three to four times a week, I had to gulp an increasing amount of sinus medicine. At home, I'd spend hours in bed each time a headache came on.

I also had severe hay fever allergies, and I saw a doctor twice a year who specialized in treating them. She prescribed Allegra. During one of my regular office visits, I mentioned that, in addition to my regular allergy symptoms, I also got severe headaches several times a week. After asking me more about them, she surprised me by saying, "I don't think they're sinus headaches. I think they're migraines. You should see a neurologist." Mom had always told me that my headaches were sinus headaches, and I had taken her word for it.

When I got home, I researched migraines on the Internet, and, sure enough, my symptoms fit the description. For the first time, I realized that Mom and I hadn't been getting sinus headaches all these years. We'd actually been suffering with migraines. A few days later, I had my first appointment with a neurologist. After I described my symptoms, he confirmed that I suffered from migraines, and he said, "When you get a headache, just take nine Advils." *Nine Advils!* His prescription shocked me, but I didn't question it. The next day, when I felt a migraine headache coming on, I got out a bottle of Advil and took nine of them.

After several hours, my headache went away, but the next day my headache returned even stronger. What I eventually discovered was that the more medicine I took, the more I suffered from rebound headaches. Rebound headaches are caused by long-term overuse of medication to treat migraines. Now, I was getting severe migraines more often, and each one lasted longer. When I went back to the neurologist and explained that my migraines were getting worse instead of better, he suggested that I would be better off seeing someone who specialized in treating headaches.

He referred me to a kindly neurologist who ran a clinic dedicated to caring for severe headache patients like me. After taking my history and examining me, she put me on new medication designed to treat migraines.

The medication worked wonders, and I thought my migraines were a thing of the past. Unfortunately, after a few weeks, the medicine stopped working, and my migraines returned as strong and debilitating as ever. Discouraged, I went back my new neurologist. She said reassuringly, "Don't worry. There's plenty of other medications we can try."

And so she wrote out another prescription. I didn't know then that I was beginning a long, frustrating ride on a medication merry-go-round that would last for the next several years. I would fill a new prescription, it would stop working after a few weeks, my headaches would return worse than ever, and I'd go back to her for another remedy.

I constantly had to fill and refill the small pill case I carried in my purse with a different cocktail of drugs. I took daily tablets to prevent migraines, something different once I started to get a migraine, pain relievers if the headache became unbearable, and nausea medication to calm my stomach so I wouldn't throw up because of the intense pain.

I was terrified that I would leave my pill case at home or lose it and have no way to relieve the pain if a migraine came on suddenly when I was away.

What I never thought about each time I tried a different combination of medicines, was that I was also subjecting my body to a plethora of side effects from these powerful drugs.

CHAPTER 49

Brain Surgery

EVEN WITH ALL THE MEDICATION, MY HEADaches did not diminish, and they made it harder and harder for me to function on a daily basis. During an office visit, my "headache" neurologist mentioned that she had just met a doctor who was trying a new surgery that might help me. I immediately made an appointment to see him at the Georgetown University Hospital in Washington, D.C.

I barely understood the surgical procedure he was describing. He called it nerve decompression surgery. He said he would microscopically separate the nerves at the base of my skull by cutting tight tunnels around each nerve to decompress them. That way, when the nerves become swollen due to a migraine, they would have room to expand without touching each other and causing pain. The doctor also said that once my incisions healed, I could come back for a second surgery to decompress or separate the nerves on the front of the brain across my forehead.

I agreed to the short operation, even though the thought of brain surgery made me nervous. There were also all the complications that I could face if something went wrong: blood clots, stroke, major mood changes, etc. I worried about how our quiet lives would be turned upside down if I woke up with uncontrollable, violent mood swings. Despite the risks, I agreed to the surgery anyway. Taking a bunch of pills to relieve my increasingly painful migraines hadn't really been working, and I was desperate for any approach that could help me.

In early 2007, at age 45, I was one of the first 350 people in the world to undergo this new procedure. When I woke up after the operation, my eyes were grotesquely black and blue. Luckily, I had big sunglasses with me. I joked with Doug that if he didn't take good care of me during my recovery, I would take off my sunglasses in public and tell people that he was the one who gave me two black eyes!

As I recovered, I noticed a marked decrease in pain where my nerves had been separated at the base of my skull. Emboldened by the results, I arranged to have a second nerve decompression surgery two months later to separate the brain nerves running along my forehead. After both surgeries, I was delighted by how much my pain decreased, but unfortunately, as the years passed my migraines slowly returned to their pre-surgery intensity.

My surgeon explained that even though the nerves had been separated, they often grew back together over time, requiring additional surgeries to re-separate them. I was devastated. No one had mentioned this possibility to me. When I underwent my brain surgeries, I thought the pain relief would be permanent.

While mulling over whether I really wanted more brain surgery, a friend told me about a new non-surgical device to treat migraines called the *Cefaly* that she'd just heard about on the news. It was already being used successfully in Europe and had just been authorized for use in the U.S. After talking it over with my neurologist, she enthusiastically agreed to send a prescription for the device to the European manufacturer. Within days, my *Cefaly* arrived. It was a metal halo that you placed around your forehead just above your eyes, attached by a sticky electrode pad in the middle. Doug loved it. He said I looked just like Xena, TV's warrior princess.

After I attached the halo to the electrode and turned it on, it made my whole forehead vibrate with electrical impulses. The theory was that these impulses would stimulate the large cranial trigeminal nerve that caused most migraines, reducing their frequency and intensity. After getting at least some relief after using the strange device, I decided that I'd much rather attach a halo to my forehead instead of getting more surgery and more black eyes.

CHAPTER 50

Side Effects

I HAD MY FIRST OF TWO SERIOUS BOUTS WITH kidney stones in 2009. I was in Raleigh, North Carolina, at a women's basketball tournament with my good friend Marni McNeese, supporting our beloved University of Maryland Terrapins as members of its booster club. The terrapin is a small edible turtle native to Maryland. At games, people wear shirts and wave banners that say, "Fear the turtle." Why would any opposing team be afraid of turtles?

The day of the championship game, we decided to kill time by taking a campus tour of North Carolina State University. I was already dressed for the game in my red women's basketball tee shirt and matching red cowboy hat. A half hour into the tour, I was suddenly doubled over by a stabbing pain in my right abdomen that radiated to my lower back. "What's wrong?" Marni asked. She had seen me deal with daily pain from both muscle spasms and migraines for years, but she immediately sensed this was more serious. "I don't know," I panted, as I struggled to stand up. "I think I need to go to the hospital."

I staggered with Marni to the nearest campus building and asked a group of students where the hospital was. One of them laughed and said, "Right across the street," as she pointed to Duke University Hospital, easily visible from our location.

I smiled through the pain. Duke was our biggest rival. Now, I thought, as I touched the Terrapin logo on the front of my red cowboy hat, "I hope the doctors at Duke will take good care of me even though I'm a Maryland fan."

When I checked in at the emergency department, the nurse gave me a bag in case my intense pain made me vomit. I was becoming more nauseous by the minute, but thankfully, I didn't throw up. When I finally saw the doctor and described my symptoms, he ordered a CT scan. After looking at the images, he said I had several large stones in both kidneys that probably wouldn't be able to pass through my body on their own because they were too big. He said I would need additional treatment once I got home and advised me to schedule an appointment with a urologist as soon as possible.

"What about the game tonight? Can I still go?" I begged the doctor.

"Well, yes, you can go," he said apprehensively, "as long as you can handle the pain. I can give you enough pain medicine to last until you get home tomorrow." Before I left the hospital, Marni took a picture of me with my doctor. I am smiling, hooked up to an IV—and resplendent in my Maryland Terrapin gear.

A week after we returned from Raleigh, I had the first of two lithotripsy treatments to break up some of my kidney stones, although many still remain embedded inside my body and could flare up at any time.

Tragically, that was the last tournament Marni and I ever traveled to. Due to long-term liver disease, she underwent a liver transplant in early 2010. She was plagued by complications and died in her sleep the day after Thanksgiving.

I had more kidney stone trouble in 2017. It was so serious, that I had to undergo a three-hour operation to remove more kidney stones. I've since learned that Topamax, which I took for many years to control my migraines, can cause kidney stones.

During the spring of 2014, my ophthalmologist broke the news to me that I needed cataract surgery in both eyes. I was just 52. Most of the people I knew who underwent cataract surgery were in their 60s or 70s. I asked, "Aren't I kind of young for that?" She said, "Sometimes it happens." After my exam, she gave me some literature about the surgery. In large print, the brochure listed steroid use as one of the top three causes of cataracts.

Steroids. I couldn't believe it. For years, I always carried steroid pills with me in case I got a migraine headache so bad that nothing else would touch it.

I hated taking steroids, but often I had no choice. I hated the way they caused me to sweat profusely and gain so much weight. Every time I picked up a new prescription, a sheet of paper was stapled to the bag with all kinds of information in tiny print about what the medication was used for and possible side effects. I never bothered to read them. I just swallowed the medicine and hoped it would work.

After I was diagnosed with cataracts, kidney stones, tremors, and eventually bipolar, I actually started to read the pharmacy information about the side effects of each prescription. I realized that many of the medications that I had taken over the years could have caused or worsened my other health conditions.

In addition, many of the medications that I took to alleviate my migraines were actually designed to treat a variety of other things, including mental health conditions like bipolar, which I was first diagnosed with in 2014. I wonder now, if all the dozens and dozens of medications I took for over 40 years could have altered my brain chemistry and led to some of the serious mental health issues I have now.

I also wonder what impact two brain surgeries had on my overall health. When I signed the consent forms for my first nerve decompression operation in 2007, they listed all kinds of possible side effects, like mood swings or loss of brain function. Could they have been the root of my bipolar?

Or was it genetic, inherited like my race or the color of my eyes? Or was it triggered by medication side effects, surgeries, physical and emotional trauma, or a combination of factors?

What I do know is that cerebral palsy, migraines and bipolar all originate in the brain: proof that a lot of my misery did indeed start in my head.

PART SEVEN:

From Top to Bottom and Back Up Again

CHAPTER 51

Blurry Vision

BY 2014, MY CHILDHOOD DIAGNOSIS OF "MILD CP" didn't feel mild at all. Even though I was only 52, I struggled to stand up, and I tottered around with painful and stiff joints like someone much older. My hands worked fine, although increasing spasticity in my fingers made it harder for me do fine motor skills like holding a pen or opening a bag of chips. This puzzled me since I have always been told that cerebral palsy was not a degenerative disease like muscular dystrophy or multiple sclerosis. I found a quote from RN Diane Walker that gave me a clue toward understanding my steady physical decline. "Although CP is not degenerative, a lifetime of fighting physical impairment can mean that people with CP often start feeling the effects of aging earlier."

Adults with cerebral palsy are also at an increased risk for mental health disorders, as I would soon experience, compared to adults without the condition, according to a 2019 study published in the *Annals of Internal Medicine* by Daniel Whitney, Ph.D. and Mark Peterson, Ph.D., M.S., FACSM, professors of physical medicine and rehabilitation at Michigan Medicine at the university in Ann Arbor. During the first half of the year, I was on top of the world. My marriage and my family were in a great place. My work with the Maryland Alliance of Disability Commissions was rewarding. Then suddenly, that summer, the bottom fell out.

July 1, 2014
Doug and I were in Long Island to visit Nilsa, my friend of over 30 years, and her family. Nilsa was nearing 70 and still working as a comptroller, and her husband David was retired. Their son Ivan had retired from the NYPD and was working as a federal marshal. Their daughter Frances taught forensics at a local high school and had two teenage children of her own.

I woke up that morning and couldn't see clearly. Everything was blurry. Rubbing my eyes didn't help, I couldn't see clearly out of either eye. Months ago, I had been told that eventually I would need cataract surgery, which I had been putting off. But overnight, it had become a big problem.

Doug and I were leaving the next day for Marlboro, New York, near Poughkeepsie, to visit my other best friend, Linda. As previously mentioned, I met Linda in 1984 when I started at *Fire Engineering* magazine. Linda and her second husband, Chester, now ran a successful business, Got2Lindy Dance Studios, teaching swing dancing in the Hudson Valley.

We had tickets to see *Wicked* on Broadway the following night. I had been looking forward to the show for months. Unfortunately, when the curtain went up, everything still looked blurry, but at least the music was great.

I have something called monovision. I use my left eye for distance and my right eye for reading. As soon as I returned from New York, I made an appointment for cataract surgery on my left eye. After my first cataract surgery, I could see great out of my left eye, but I still couldn't read out of my right eye for another six weeks until I had surgery on that eye.

By the end of August, after my second cataract operation, I could finally see clearly out of both eyes. Almost as soon as my vision cleared up, I began to experience drastic mood swings and found myself growing increasingly, and inexplicably, irritable.

At the same time, I was diagnosed with a severe urinary tract infection (UTI). The first round of antibiotics didn't clear it up; it only got worse. Doug took a picture of my skin, which was beet red from the infection. I went back to the doctor for more antibiotics. Unbeknownst to me, my UTI only added to my mental confusion. Research shows that younger people who get UTI's experience physical symptoms like painful urination, while older people who get UTI's may show increased signs of confusion, agitation, or withdrawal. At 52, I was now firmly in the latter category.

CHAPTER 52

Searching For Answers

I FELT CONFUSED ALL THE TIME AND WAS UNABLE to focus on or complete even the most basic tasks. Always super organized and goal driven, I had become the opposite of myself seemingly overnight. Words were flowing out of my mouth so quickly that Doug couldn't understand what I was saying. When I wasn't talking nonsensically, I was up all night sending long rambling emails to everyone I knew.

Doug knew I was spinning out of control and that something was drastically wrong with me, but he didn't know how to help me, and I couldn't help myself. In desperation, we drove to the hospital. After spending several hours in the emergency department, I was released around midnight, without being diagnosed or treated, which only made things worse. Doug was worried, stressed and exhausted. My condition was clearly taking a toll on him. He had never seen me this way.

As we left the hospital that night, I was convinced that the people in the lobby were talking about me.

In addition to being confused and incoherent, I was also delusional.

Two days later, and still searching for answers, Doug took me to the emergency room at a well-known Baltimore hospital.

After waiting in the emergency department for hours, I was finally ushered into a private room. Over the next couple of hours various doctors came by to examine and talk to me. One senior doctor asked, "Have you ever been diagnosed as bipolar?"

"No, never!" I said emphatically, suddenly remembering that my Aunt Joyce had struggled with bipolar herself decades earlier.

Eventually a nurse came by and said sternly, "Sheri, you have to get up right now, get out of that hospital gown, and put your clothes on if you want to walk out of here." I think she sensed that I was on the verge of being admitted to the psych ward. I did as I was told, and then Doug came in and said, "Let's go." Back home we went, once again with no answers.

CHAPTER 53

Fleeing To Frankford

BY THIS TIME, I WAS SUSPICIOUS OF EVERYONE, including Doug, and I refused to go to another hospital. I told Doug I needed some time away from him, and I begged him to take me to Patty Reid's house in Frankford, Delaware, not far from Bethany Beach. I remained close to Patty even after Kerry (her husband and my mentor) died in 2006.

We arrived at Patty's unannounced, which we had never done. Patty and her daughters Heather and Logan, were shocked to see us, but they invited us in. They could see right away that I wasn't in my right mind; I was rambling and talking very loudly and excitedly. Doug tried to explain what was going on, and he said that he wanted to leave me there. Patty, who had enough health problems of her own, was left to deal with me in a state she had never seen me in.

All I remember of that horrible day and night is that Doug left for what he thought would be a few days of peace. I hadn't slept for days, and I told Patty that I just wanted to go to sleep upstairs in the guest bedroom. What I didn't know was that the room wasn't ready for guests because it was under repair. Logan or Heather hastily put sheets on the bed anyway and got the room ready for me. I don't remember whether I ever slept, but I do know that I had brought several framed pictures of family and friends with me so that I could look at them during the night. Maybe I was trying to hold onto some semblance of reality as I placed them around the guest bedroom.

Sometime during the night, I lost my ability to speak. I remember trying to form words that wouldn't come out. Patty said, "Sheri, I don't think I can help you."

Desperate, Patty retrieved my phone and called my friend Linda in New York and put me on the phone. As soon as Linda heard me speak, she knew something was seriously wrong. She had known me for 30 years and had never heard me like this. Alarmed, she asked to speak to Patty, whom she didn't even know. The two of them somehow got in touch with my neurologist who suggested Patty call 911 to get me to the local hospital.

The ambulance took me to a small community hospital in Maryland, just south of the Delaware state line. In the emergency department, several tests, including a CT scan, were performed to make sure there was nothing physically wrong with me. Since the hospital didn't have a psych ward, I was admitted to a private room.

Linda raced down from New York to be with me, and she and Patty took turns staying in the room. I was still paranoid and didn't want anyone in my family there. Whenever Linda or Patty suggested they call Doug or my sister, Kim, to come, I would insist I didn't want them there. They respected my wishes but secretly kept Doug and Kim informed.

The problem, they told me later, was that there was little to report. The hospital was ill-equipped for mental-health problems and, since I had been admitted on a weekend, the single psychiatrist on staff was unavailable.

Linda, who spent hours at my side, said that most of the doctors who came to see me concluded that I was bipolar. Linda admitted to them that I was certainly in a manic state, but that in all the years she had known me, worked with me and lived with me, she had never witnessed me displaying any signs of mental illness. She wanted them to check the records of my two recent emergency room visits, but they said they liked to do their own diagnosis. They noted that one of the drugs I was taking for my migraines, Seroquel, is also used to treat bipolar, and they told Linda that I probably had mental health issues I had never told her about. She urged them to call my neurologist, which they finally did. During the call, my neurologist reiterated that she had only treated me for migraines and had only prescribed Seroquel for that purpose. She also stressed that she had never seen me display any signs of a mental health disorder.

It didn't help that I was still talking non-stop and, with my advocacy background, was insisting to know the qualifications of the doctors who came in to see me, which they took as a personal affront. Since I had been admitted as a psychiatric patient, 24 hours a day, someone was stationed at a desk just outside my room to keep an eye on me.

Finally, on Monday, the psychiatrist came in to see me. When he found out that I was under the care of a neurologist, he, too, assumed that I was taking 100 mg of Seroquel daily because I was bipolar. He immediately upped the dosage to 600 mg per day, which made me incredibly thirsty; I felt dehydrated and kept asking for more water. I gulped down water as fast as the nurses could bring it. No matter how much water I drank, I still wanted more.

After days at my side, Linda and Patty had to go back to their lives, so they asked Kim and Doug to come relieve them. For decades, I had taken so many different medications to alleviate my painful, debilitating migraines, that Doug was convinced that my mental condition had been caused by too much medication and had nothing to do with bipolar. He insisted that I needed to be admitted to a detox facility in Florida, and he was making all the arrangements for me to go down there for treatment.

Finally, after nearly a week lying in bed, guzzling water and talking nonstop, I told my desk watcher that I wanted to leave my room and walk to the hospital chapel. As I followed her to the small chapel, I felt my mind clearing. I will be forever grateful to the chaplain on duty for praying with me that day. As he prayed, I finally felt some peace. As soon as Doug came to visit later that day, I told him to dial up the detox facility in Florida so that I could tell them I wasn't coming.

I was discharged the following day with a week's worth of Seroquel and told to follow up with outpatient psychiatric treatment.

Since the hospital was not far from the beach, which I've always loved, I begged Doug to get a hotel room with an ocean view for just one night. I was convinced I just needed a night in beautiful surroundings, so that I could recover. I guess Doug grasped at this hope, and for a small fortune, he found us a great room with an ocean view. After a peaceful night, we headed home.

CHAPTER 54

If Only

IF ONLY I HAD LISTENED TO MY DOCTOR'S ADVICE and followed up with psychiatric treatment, then maybe I wouldn't have ended up in my local hospital's behavioral health unit, unofficially called the psych ward.

Back home, after taking the prescribed 600 mg of Seroquel for a few days, I was too dehydrated to take the rest. I threw the remaining pills in the trash and proclaimed myself cured. I refused to believe I was bipolar. I chalked up my mental breakdown to too much stress and too much medication.

My friends—who had kept in constant contact with Doug—were relieved. Never having known me in such a state, they were happy to believe that whatever it was had passed, and the Sheri they knew was back. Doug was just happy to have me home. I convinced him and everyone, including myself, that I was fine. And I *was* better for a brief time.

My urinary tract infection had only gotten worse in the hospital, and so I went back to the doctor at urgent care. In addition to giving me another round of antibiotics, he diagnosed me with water intoxication, brought on because I had been drinking an excessive amount of water to quench my thirst from taking too much Seroquel. He told me to monitor my water intake.

Severe cases of water intoxication can cause seizures, coma and even death. Another symptom is mental confusion. As noted earlier, urinary tract infections in older adults can also cause mental confusion.

So, there I was, in total mental meltdown, being buffeted by water intoxication, bipolar and a urinary tract infection, all at the same time. Increasingly out of my mind, I lashed out at the one person who loved me above all else, my husband Douglas. And then, I did the unthinkable. I gave away my beloved dog, Asha, who I had rescued in 2010.

Two days before giving away Asha, I had become uncontrollably angry and ordered Doug out of the house. He was afraid, exhausted, and frustrated. He didn't know what to do, and thought the best way to defuse the situation was to follow my wishes and leave. He left me alone with Asha and took some money and clothes and checked into a hotel around the corner from his office near D.C. In a moment of anger, he turned off his phone so I couldn't reach him.

When we moved into our condo, we decided not to get a landline and just use our cell phones.

Alone and increasingly frantic, I couldn't find my phone charger. Doug wasn't answering his phone. I was terrified that my battery would run out, trapping me inside with Asha, with no way to reach out for help.

The next morning, I woke up convinced that I could no longer feed or walk Asha and that she would die trapped inside our home with me unless I found someone to take care of her. Disheveled and disoriented, I took Asha outside desperately looking for someone to take her.

As I stood in front of my condo building, holding Asha's leash in my hand as she waited patiently beside me, I spotted a young couple delivering newspapers. I walked up to them and stammered, "Do you like dogs?" "Yes," the young man said, surprised to be asked such an unusual question. "Well, I need someone to take care of my dog, because I can't. Can you follow me inside? I'll give you her food and treats to take with you."

Unquestioning, they followed me inside. As I handed over my dog, her treats and her food, I said, "Let me give you some money to take care of her." They waited while I got my checkbook and wrote out a check for $1000. I left the name blank, and handed it to the young man.

Delusional, I believed that Asha wouldn't be safe with Doug either. "One more thing," I said sternly, "whatever you do, even if my husband, Douglas

Spandau, comes looking for her, don't give her back to him. He'll hurt her. Promise me, you won't give her back to him." The young man nodded yes. Then I handed over Asha and watched him put her into the back seat of his car and drive away.

CHAPTER 55

Where's Asha

Giving away my precious dog, who I treated like my baby, was the clearest sign of how sick I was that day.

With Asha gone, I began frantically knocking on the doors in my building. When no one answered, I did the same thing in the building next door. Unfortunately, the few neighbors I knew had all recently moved away. With no luck inside the condos, I staggered back out to the parking lot and flagged down a passing car. When the woman in the passenger seat rolled down her window, I incoherently said I needed help. When the startled woman went to close her window, I said angrily, "Well, if you won't help me, then you can take this!" I threw my cell phone at her through the open window. Frightened, the woman closed her window as her husband sped away.

I only have fragmented memories of what happened next. I went back inside my condo and asked God to put me out of my misery. The thought of taking my own life never crossed my mind, but I pleaded over and over, "God, just let me go to sleep and never wake up." Before I went to bed, I wrote a note, signed and dated it, and then placed it on top of our desk, along with my license and a copy of my will.

Apparently, the people I threw my phone at in the parking lot must have called the police and gave them my phone. Not long after I had laid down, there was a knock at my door. I opened it to see three police officers. As they came inside, I sat frightened in my living room recliner while they figured out what to do next. One of the officers found my note, will and license on the desk.

Eventually, they asked me to stand up and put my hands behind my back. For the first time in my life, I was put in handcuffs. For weeks afterwards, I was scarred by the pain, both physical and mental, of those handcuffs.

I was placed in the front seat of a police SUV and driven to a local ER. After being evaluated for a couple hours to make sure that there was nothing physically wrong with me, doctors told Doug, who had arrived at the hospital after being contacted by the police at work, that I would be admitted to the behavioral health unit, or psych ward.

The behavioral health unit is a locked, secure unit that cares for psychiatric patients on an inpatient or outpatient basis, anywhere from a few days to a few weeks. The fluorescently-lit unit has a row of patient rooms on each end of the unit with a large open space in the middle for activities and dining. A phone mounted on the wall, for patients to make and receive calls, has a short metal cord to the receiver so that the caller can't strangle themselves. Aides are constantly walking around and monitoring you every second. There is no privacy.

Two patients are assigned to each concrete-walled room, which has no clock or TV. Beside each bed is an old wooden table with open-ended shelves underneath to put clothes or a few personal items. Shoelaces, belts, or drawstrings are not permitted. You can't have a cell phone. No visitor is allowed in your room. Each twin bed is topped with the thinnest white sheet, blanket and pillow imaginable.

Intercom announcements call you to come for meals, group sessions or for your medication, which is dispensed by a nurse who watches to make sure you take it. Patients wear paper blue scrubs or regular clothes if a visitor brings them. Every patient is assigned a psychiatrist, social worker and a nurse. Visitation is limited to one hour in the evening during the week or two hours on Saturday and Sunday.

The first day I was there, I read through the contents of a white folder that had been left on the table beside my bed. I was shocked and devastated to read the page which listed my diagnosis: *bipolar with delusions*. I cried every night and told God that I couldn't handle being physically disabled *and* mentally ill.

Some people are voluntarily committed for 48 or 72 hours, which means that they can leave after that period if doctors determine that they are stable enough to leave. I, on the other hand, was admitted involuntarily, which meant that I would stay until doctors determined that I was no longer a danger to myself or others.

I thought of all the old movies I had seen where husbands had committed their wives to mental institutions against their will, even if they weren't mentally ill, and kept them locked up for life.

Fortunately for me, it was 2014, and I was in a place that provided only short-term psychiatric care, which meant that I could only be kept there for a few weeks.

After I was admitted to the psych ward, Doug finally returned home and was alarmed when Asha wasn't there to greet him. When he called and told the nurses that Asha was missing, one of them asked me what had happened to the dog. I told her that I had given Asha to a couple delivering newspapers in our building.

Meanwhile, Doug had called my sister Kim to let her know I had been admitted. She drove down with my niece Alicia who insisted on coming to see me. I wish I could have spared her from having to visit me in the psych ward.

Doug was frantic to find our dog. He conferred with Linda who made lost dog signs and emailed them to Doug to post. With little to go on, he called the publisher of our weekly community newspaper and explained the situation. Miraculously, newspaper staff members tracked down the couple who had been delivering newspapers in our building that morning. Since I had told them not to give Asha back to Doug, they refused to return her. My sister tried to explain the situation to them to no avail. At his wit's end, Doug contacted the police for help. One of our neighbors stepped forward and told the police how much Doug loved our dog and how well he treated her.

The police agreed to accompany Doug to meet the couple who had our dog. After a brief meeting, the couple was finally persuaded to hand over a tired, hungry and confused Asha back to her overjoyed Daddy. Doug thanked them for taking care of our dog. He let them cash the $1,000 check that I had given them, saying it was the least he could do.

CHAPTER 56

Denial

TWO WEEKS LATER, I WAS RELEASED UNDER Doug's care, and the following day I began an intensive daily outpatient program back at the hospital, in a suite of rooms connected to the psych ward I had just been released from.

For the next two weeks, from 8:30 a.m. to 3 p.m., I attended group therapy under the supervision of psychiatrists, nurses, social workers and therapists. There were about 12 to 14 of us on any given day.

We represented a cross section of ages, races and socioeconomic backgrounds: an 18-year-old kid with a traumatic brain injury, a woman whose husband had committed suicide, a young mother who worked part time as a school photographer. There was even a rocket scientist. Some of us had homes, jobs and families who loved us. Others were single with no family or support. And some were homeless.

Some, like me, were new to psychiatric hospitalization and had never been part of an outpatient program. Others were old hands, and had been hospitalized or part of the outpatient program several times. Every morning new outpatients joined us. Every afternoon people were discharged from the program to make room for new patients.

Returning patients were greeted with "Welcome back (name)!" like they were long, lost friends. Whenever I heard "Welcome back" I cringed and told myself that I was different, "I'll never be admitted to a psych ward again."

One of the things all of us patients wrestled with was how to tell other people about our mental health conditions. During group therapy we were told we shouldn't be afraid or ashamed to share our diagnosis with others. My reaction was, "It's one thing to tell people that I was hospitalized for a knee replacement or for a heart condition. It's a whole other thing to say, I am bipolar, and I just got out of the psych ward."

During my outpatient treatment, all of the doctors, nurses, social workers and therapists were caring and dedicated and gave us the tools to avoid rehospitalization. Some of us listened, and others, like me, didn't.

After two weeks of daily sessions, I "graduated" from the outpatient program and was no longer required to go to daily sessions. I was told to follow up with both a therapist and a psychiatrist, who could manage my medications. Doug found a therapist at a local counseling center, and I went to one appointment. Linda, who was still helping Doug from New York as much as she could, had googled extensively to find a psychiatrist she thought would be a good fit for me. Doug made an appointment with the psychiatrist Linda found in Columbia, Dr. Angela Onwuanibe.

I had never had a problem trusting any of the doctors who treated my myriad of physical conditions. Now, however, I was unwilling to let this new doctor help me, even though she was perfectly qualified to treat my mental health condition.

During our session the following week, instead of listening to what she was telling me, I told myself, "I can't wait to get out of here and be done with psychiatry. Since I'm not bipolar, I don't need to waste my time seeing a therapist, a psychiatrist, or taking medication for a condition I don't have." I was still in denial.

CHAPTER 57

Just Going Through the Motions

AFTER MY ONE VISIT TO DR. ONWUANIBE, I stopped taking my meds and never bothered to refill the prescription. I spent the next five years just going through the motions of living.

Although I continued to serve on the Maryland Alliance of Disability Commissions, I disconnected socially. I was too embarrassed to go back to church, even though the assistant minister had taken the time to visit me in the psych ward. I was afraid to talk about my condition. I saw family and friends only when it was absolutely necessary. I made excuses about why I couldn't see them more often and told everyone I was fine when they asked.

Prior to 2014, we frequently spent weekends at my Mom or Kim's house. Now, when I knew I had to visit, we'd leave early in the morning, Doug would drive two hours to our destination, we'd spend a few hours, and then turn around and drive another two hours back home.

I spent those years watching TV to pass the time. I usually only left the house to take my dog Asha for a quick walk when Doug was at work or to go to the health club with Doug on Saturday mornings. I hid my seclusion from my family by telling them stories of all the things I was doing, which in reality I wasn't doing at all.

Outwardly, things appeared normal. Inwardly, I was just fooling myself and everyone else.

CHAPTER 58

One Crisis Leads to Another

MOM AND HER THIRD HUSBAND DOM (SHORT for Domenick), now in their early 80s, had been living in their senior community in Mount Laurel, NJ for 25 years. Dom had been in failing health for years and had been diagnosed with COPD, brought on by years of smoking.

Dom's sole focus was to make sure Mom was taken care of. The house had recently been painted. The kitchen and a bathroom had been redone. A new heating/air conditioning unit had been installed. He even bought a new car so Mom wouldn't have to worry about repairs. All the receipts were organized in a binder in the garage, records from 25 years of marriage.

Now, Mom said, he slept most of the day in his recliner and only went out on Wednesday mornings to grocery shop. My mom, on the other hand, was still physically active. Twice a week, she did water aerobics, even teaching it in the summer, line danced, and ushered at the Walnut Theater in Philadelphia.

As Dom's health worsened, Kim and I stepped up our visits to Mount Laurel. One weekend, she would drive from Pennsylvania to check up on them, and the next weekend Doug and I would drive up from Maryland early Saturday morning and spend a few hours with them before beginning the long drive back home.

At 10 p.m. on Saturday, March 16, 2019 the phone rang. I started to panic when I saw "MOTHER" on the caller ID. She had never called me on a Saturday night; we always talked on Tuesday mornings. I took a deep breath and tried to sound cheerful, "Hello Mom. What's up?"

"Sheri. I'm sorry to call you so late, but Dom said he wants me to take him to the hospital, and I don't know what to do," she said anxiously. "Mom, I'm glad you called. It's OK," I said, hoping to sound reassuring. "You know, Dom has been sleeping most of the day now, she continued, "and he doesn't have much energy. After we came back from getting our taxes done this morning, he started telling me he needed to go to the hospital. I don't know why he wants to go or what they can do for him. He just sleeps most of the day," she repeated, not realizing she had just said that.

"Mom, if he wakes up tomorrow morning and still wants you to take him to the hospital, go ahead and take him to the ER. Call me before you go. I love you," I sighed as I hung up.

As soon as I hung up the phone, I called my sister Kim. I recounted my conversation with Mom and told her I would keep her updated.

The next morning, even though I had been up and worrying since 6 a.m., I waited until 10 to call Mom. When she didn't answer, I knew something was wrong. I called their local hospital and found out that Mom and Dom were in the ER waiting for Dom to be admitted. I immediately sensed two things. One, that I had to leave immediately to be with Mom. And secondly, I feared that Dom would never be coming back home. I redialed my sister and told her that I was leaving for New Jersey immediately to stay with Mom while Dom was in the hospital.

I stayed with Mom two weeks, and we visited Dom every day. Since I was now with her constantly, I noticed that she was repeating the same things, even during the same conversation. For the first few days, I chalked it up to old age. But I soon realized that things were much more serious than I had thought. One night I opened the refrigerator and saw food that was unsafe to eat, months past the expiration dates. I found blood pressure medicine that Mom was supposed to be taking every day but wasn't taking at all. I let her drive us to her aerobics class on Tuesday morning. She found the YMCA okay, but during the class, she had trouble following the teacher's instructions. Afterward, in the parking lot, she looked around in confusion, struggling to find her car. That night I called Kim and told her that no matter what happened with Dom, it wasn't safe for Mom to live on her own. We both hung up in tears.

Since Dom's ex-wife had Alzheimer's and was already living in an assisted living facility, I called one of his daughters who told me that her Mom had undergone testing at a geriatric neurology center in North Jersey. She gave me the details, and I called and made an appointment for Mom on April 10.

Meanwhile doctors suspected that Dom had cancer and they wanted to do a colonoscopy, but Dom's heart was too weak to undergo the procedure. They said there was nothing more they could do for him. When he was stable enough, he was transferred to a local rehab facility to give my sister time to find an assisted living facility for both Mom and Dom near her home in Pennsylvania.

Mom's brother Ed, who had joined Kim and me at the hospital, entertained us with funny jokes and stories. We all laughed uproariously, but I was laughing the loudest and talking even faster, not realizing that I was cycling into the manic phase of another bipolar episode.

A few days later, things with Mom went from bad to really bad. That morning, a hospital social worker called to go over some details about Dom. When I answered the phone and started talking to the social worker, Mom went berserk because she thought I was trying to take over Dom's care instead of letting her take charge.

After I hung up, I told Mom that I had to finish getting dressed so that we could get to the hospital. While I was in the bedroom, Mom stormed out of the house without telling me. When I came out and found her missing, I panicked. I looked outside, up and down the street, anywhere I could think of, but I still couldn't find her. Doug was due from Maryland any minute. When he arrived, we drove all around the neighborhood looking for her to no avail. Now Doug and I were both panicked. We were on the verge of calling the police but decided to go back to the house first in case she had walked back there.

When we opened the door, we were relieved to see that she had found her way home. Mom, however, was angrier that I had ever seen her. Instead of saying hello to Doug, she sneered, "I never want to see you or Doug again."

We were devastated. Doug decided we had to take Mom to Kim's house for her safety. Doug said, "Let's go, Carol." Mom got in our car because she thought we were taking her back to the hospital to see Dom. When she realized that we on the way to Kim's house instead, she sat in the back and angrily cried the whole way there.

The next day, Kim took Mom to a local doctor and discovered that Mom's blood pressure was dangerously high because she hadn't been taking her blood pressure medication. Kim took over Mom's care and drove her back and forth to New Jersey to visit Dom while checking out nearby assisted living facilities. On April 10, Kim drove Mom up to North Jersey to get tested. Afterward, doctors told Kim that Mom was showing some of the classic symptoms of Alzheimer's.

Those next few weeks were hard on Kim because Mom seethed with anger. She constantly berated Kim, "How dare you make decisions for me!" I kept reminding Kim that she was doing the right thing by keeping Mom safe while looking for the best place for both Mom and Dom.

Kim found a great assisted living facility just 15 minutes from her house, where Mom and Dom could live together in the same apartment. I can never thank my sister enough for what she did for Mom and Dom.

A few weeks after Mom's neurological testing in North Jersey, Kim received a written report from the team of doctors there. They concluded that Mom did have Alzheimer's and supported our decision to move her into assisted living. One thing in the report surprised us. They said that Mom had probably had Alzheimer's for at least two years before we first noticed the symptoms. Mom had done a remarkable job hiding her condition from us.

CHAPTER 59

Unraveling

As soon as I returned home, I started to unravel. I didn't realize that stress can trigger a bipolar episode. The stress of dealing with Mom's newly-diagnosed Alzheimer's and Dom's terminal condition, combined with the fact that I had stopped taking medication to control my condition years before, created the perfect storm for another mental collapse.

The first thing I noticed was that I had trouble focusing. Normally laser focused, I couldn't concentrate on a book or on a TV show. So, instead, after dinner, when Doug and I normally watched our favorite shows, I made an excuse and retreated to bed early, hoping sleep would bring peace to my troubled mind. Depression surrounded me like a heavy cloud.

We were both concerned that I was having another mental breakdown, and Doug desperately tried everything to "snap" me out it. He brought me my favorite foods, recorded comedies to watch, and urged me to go for walks around our condo development, with its panoramic water view of a small tributary that flowed all the way to the Chesapeake Bay.

In hindsight, I wish that I had put the pieces together at the first sign of trouble and reached out to Dr. Onwuanibe, the psychiatrist I visited in 2014, so that she could have put me back on the right medication. Unfortunately, my mind was too fractured to think clearly.

My sister Kim called every day to try and talk me out of my deepening depression. She continuously texted me with positive, spiritually uplifting messages. As I struggled to read all of them, I prayed to God and begged him to heal me.

I increasingly thought about ending my life so that I wouldn't have to live with a mind that couldn't function. I thought that Doug and my family and friends would be better off without me. I didn't tell Doug how I was really feeling. I knew if I did, he'd try to stop me from executing my plan.

June 14, 2019
I had filled my monthly prescription for sleeping pills and took all 30 of them together before bed.

When Doug couldn't wake me the next morning, he called an ambulance. I woke up at our local hospital with Doug at my side, terrified that I'd be sent back to the same psych ward that had treated me in 2014.

One of the psychiatric therapists who had treated me five years earlier came to see me. I refused to admit that I had attempted suicide. At the end of her visit, she recommended that I go to a local psychiatric outpatient clinic the following week.

I was released the next day with a diagnosis of *aphasia*, which made no sense to me. I later learned that aphasia is defined as a loss of ability to understand or express speech, caused by brain damage. Well, I did have brain damage at birth, and when I arrived at the hospital after taking 30 sleeping pills, I was out of it and unable to speak, but I certainly didn't have aphasia. I was bipolar, even though I wasn't ready to admit it.

My attending doctor sent me home with a prescription for Topamax, a medicine that I had previously taken to prevent migraines, and which is sometimes used to treat bipolar. For some reason, he didn't prescribe Depakote, which was the medicine that had stabilized me in that same hospital in 2014.

CHAPTER 60

Fractured

When Doug and I left the hospital, we were just grateful that I hadn't been readmitted to the psych ward.

The following Monday, Doug drove me to the local outpatient clinic. We were told to be there by 10 a.m. so that we could be assigned to a psychiatrist. Because I was so freaked out about going, we arrived there late, and I was told that there were no more slots available. We drove right back home.

The Topamax did nothing to help me. I continued to get more delusional and refused to get out of bed. I started to talk incoherently. Doug was at his wits end. He phoned my neurologist. Then he called my sister Kim who overheard me talking incoherently. She urged Doug to take me to a nearby psychiatric hospital that had an emergency walk-in clinic.

Soon after we arrived, a psychiatrist came out to speak to us in the waiting room. I was disheveled and clearly incoherent. Doug had resigned himself, as much as it devastated him, to the fact that I needed to be re-hospitalized. The psychiatrist said that she would check to see if there was a bed available in the psych ward. After a few minutes, she came back and said there were no beds available.

I was told I could come back the following week for the outpatient program where I would see a psychiatrist, get medication and attend weekday group therapy sessions. I angrily took the information, and Doug reluctantly took me back home, frustrated that he couldn't help me.

June 28, 2019
The thought of waiting even a few more days for treatment seemed impossible. I was afraid that even if I hung on until I could start the outpatient program, that it would be several more days before any medication would alleviate my symptoms.

In my fractured mind, suicide seemed like the only "logical" solution. I'd secretly been researching how to do it for weeks. I thought of using a gun to end my life, but I quickly ruled it out. I didn't have one and wouldn't know how to use it. Besides, with my spasticity, I was certain I'd screw it up and shoot the ceiling, or my dog or worse yet, maim rather than kill myself. The thought of living in a body more damaged than mine already was seemed unbearable. I settled on pills. I would swallow all of the dozens of extra strength Tylenols I had stockpiled over the years to relieve my physical pain.

After I'd been released from the hospital after my first suicide attempt a few weeks earlier, Doug had been afraid to leave me alone, much less go back work in D.C. On this particular Friday, I tricked Doug into going back to work by assuring him that it was OK to leave me alone for a few hours so that he could check in at the office.

Relieved that I had gotten away with my ruse, I smiled as I told him not to worry and then locked the door behind him. I looked at the clock. It was 8:30. I got out several bottles of extra strength Tylenol and sat down on the floor beside my bed with an open bottle of Maker's Mark whiskey to wash them all down. As I started jamming as many pills as I could fit in my mouth, I said to myself, "Soon this will all be over."

Doug quickly finished his business in D.C. and called and left me a message saying that he'd be home soon. I never heard the phone. When Doug walked in the front door just after 2 p.m., he found me unconscious with foam coming out of my mouth on the bedroom floor. I had fallen over flat on my face. I had a bleeding gash above my lower lip and an injured right arm. He tried to shake me awake, and when he couldn't, he immediately dialed 911.

As soon as the paramedics arrived, they saved my life by administering Narcan, used to reverse drug overdoses. I was rushed to a Baltimore hospital. Just before the ambulance arrived at the emergency entrance, I woke up vomiting black bile all over myself.

I thank God every day that my second suicide attempt failed. But when I arrived at the hospital that day, I was devastated I was still alive. My liver, however, was in big trouble.

The doctors informed Doug that I had taken so many pills that I was facing liver failure and a possible transplant. Despite receiving continuous IV drips of acetylcysteine to reverse the damage, my liver was not responding. The liver releases enzymes in response to damage or disease. Daily blood tests showed that my enzyme count was continuing to rise, instead of going back down.

I prayed for my liver to recover so that I wouldn't have to undergo a transplant and a lengthy recovery *before* I could even begin to receive intensive psychiatric treatment. At the same time, I felt unworthy of a new liver since I had intentionally damaged my own, and didn't want to take a liver away from someone who actually deserved one. I thought how furious my friend Marni would be. I imagined her yelling at me from above, "I needed a transplant because I had a medical condition that caused my liver to fail. You may need a transplant because you were selfish enough to try and take your own life. How dare you?"

There was no chance of escaping life now. I couldn't go anywhere because I was under a constant suicide watch. Hospital workers called "patient sitters" took

12-hour shifts in my room. Under suicide watch, I wasn't allowed to have a combination call button/TV remote attached to my bed because it had a cord. As I laid in bed watching medicine drip into my veins, I knew that as soon as my liver was healthy enough, I'd be escorted from the open door of my private room to the locked doors of the hospital's psych ward.

I was overwhelmed with guilt and shame. Whenever I saw Doug, I told him over and over how sorry I was as I cried uncontrollably.

Thankfully, my liver slowly began to recover, so I didn't end up needing a transplant. Two weeks later, my doctor said that my liver recovery was miraculous

My physical recovery was the good news. The bad news was that I was now healthy enough to begin another stint in a psych ward. I hated the thought of being locked away again under the 24-hour glare of florescent lights and unrelenting scrutiny from patients, doctors, nurses and social workers. I had no idea how long I would be locked up or when I would be released. Would I be locked away for life? Forced to wear a straightjacket or undergo electroshock treatment, strapped to a gurney as electrodes are placed on my head just before currents convulse my body? I couldn't stop myself from imagining the worst.

CHAPTER 61

A Tortuous Road To Recovery

IN JULY 2019, WHEN I LEFT THE HOSPITAL, I WAS nowhere close to being fully recovered. After my second suicide attempt, I did admit to taking an overdose of pills, but Doug and I didn't tell my attending physician that I had been previously hospitalized for bipolar. When I was diagnosed with a severe case of depression by one of the hospital's psychiatrists, I went along with it and never mentioned my previous hospitalizations.

One of the many downfalls of healthcare in America, is that there is no integrated care of the mind and body. Every part of a human being is fragmented into specialties, and doctors rely primarily on their patients to tie all their symptoms, treatments and medications together with no one looking at the big picture, or cause and effect.

During my stay in the psych ward, my liver was still in such a fragile state, my doctors didn't want to overtax it by giving me too much medication. So I was given only tiny doses at a time, which did nothing to decrease my anxiety. Instead, I was free to torment myself day and night with guilt over what I had done to myself, to Doug, and to my family.

When I had been hospitalized the first time with bipolar five years earlier, I had been given the right medication to stabilize my condition, and I recovered within six weeks.

Now that I was back home, Doug and my sister thought I'd recover the same way I had before. Only this time, I wasn't on the right medication, and I was frightened, so I stubbornly stayed under the covers and refused to go back to my psychiatrist so that she could put me back on the proper medication. Doug made an appointment for me to go see her, but I called to cancel it. As the weeks dragged on, I did nothing except get more agitated and irrational.

In September, Dom died. Kim made arrangements for the family to spend a few days in Atlantic City, one of his favorite places.

Mentally, I was in bad shape. I still hadn't seen my psychiatrist, but I wanted to be there for Mom. I haphazardly threw some things in a suitcase, made arrangements for the dog, and Doug and I headed to Atlantic City.

The trip was a disaster. Normally, Doug and I love to get away for a few days, but we barely said two words to anybody for the two days we were there. All

I wanted to do was hide out in our hotel room with Doug and ramble incessantly to him about how much trouble I was in. He couldn't take much more. I could see how much of a toll I was taking on his health, and I became increasingly frightened that something was going to happen to him, leaving me all alone.

Back home, I continued to hibernate, getting more out of control every day, until Doug, finally at his wit's end, made another appointment with my psychiatrist, Dr. Onwuabibe, for the end of October. The night before my appointment, I became so angry, incoherent and agitated, that Doug called Kim in desperation. Doug put his phone on speaker so that she could hear me. She told Doug to call 911.

When the paramedics came, I met them on the front steps of our building, agitated and rambling. After they took my vital signs, they offered to take me by ambulance back to the same Baltimore Hospital I had been released from three months earlier. One of the paramedics said, "The decision is up to you, but if you refuse, and 911 is called again, the police will come and take you back to the hospital in handcuffs." I stood there even more terrified, suddenly remembering how I'd been taken from my home in handcuffs during my first bipolar episode in 2014.

By this time Doug and I were both trembling. Doug looked me in the eye and said, "Please, Sheri. Just wait one more day, and let me take you back to see Dr. O. Tell them to leave, and come back inside with me. Just come with me to Dr. O tomorrow. I'm begging you. Please. I love you." His words momentarily cut through my confusion long enough for me to turn back to the paramedic and say, "Thank you for coming, but I'll wait to go see my psychiatrist tomorrow." I grabbed Doug's hand and walked back inside.

The next afternoon, Doug and I arrived at my psychiatrist's office. A male nurse ushered me and Doug into an office so that he could do an initial intake. I rambled through a long nonsensical description of my condition, while Doug sat beside me turning white and sweating profusely. Finally, Doug left me alone to continue with the nurse, while he met with Dr. Onwuanibe.

I can never thank Dr. Angela Onwuanibe and her staff enough for the compassion and respect they showed us. Instead of going back to the hospital, I went home with Doug that night, armed with a prescription for the right medicine to finally restore my mental equilibrium.

This time, I took my medication as directed, and I kept my follow-up appointment with Dr. Onwuanibe. When I walked back into her office for my next appointment two weeks later, I was almost back to my old self. I even wore lipstick.

Mental health conditions can be triggered by a chemical imbalance in the brain and can be treated with medication and therapy, just like high blood pressure can be treated with medication and counseling about diet and lifestyle changes. We have no trouble talking endlessly about our physical health when we get together with family and friends, "I just went to see a new cardiologist. My husband just got diagnosed with cancer, etc." But we don't open up about our mental health. This needs to change or more people will suffer and, even more tragically, die in silence. Now, I have no problem saying that I'm bipolar or mentioning that I have an appointment with my psychiatrist.

People with mental health conditions should be treated the same way we treat those with cancer or arthritis—with respect and compassion.

Unfortunately, there are not nearly enough mental health professionals, resources or treatment options for everyone who needs them. Mental health is woefully underfunded. We must let our congressmen, senators and our local and state legislators know that funding for mental health should be increased, not decreased.

As for me, I haven't missed a day of medication or a psychiatric appointment since October 2019. I will take my medication every day and continue to see a psychiatrist for the rest of my life to monitor my mental health and adjust my medication, as needed.

For much of my life, I've felt imbalanced—both physically and mentally. Today, after embracing myself fully, I am balanced.

My husband Douglas and I are still going strong 40 years after we first met in high school gym class.

PART EIGHT:

Lessons Learned

10 Mental Health Tips I Learned The Hard Way

1. Stress is a trigger.

Stress can trigger mental health conditions. Prior to my first bipolar episode in 2014, I lost most of my vision due to cataracts, underwent two surgeries within six weeks to restore it, and developed a severe urinary tract infection that contributed to my mental confusion.

My second bipolar episode in 2019 was precipitated by my mother's Alzheimer's diagnosis. Now, I take note of when I'm under stress and take the necessary steps to manage it before things get out of control.

2. No one chooses to be depressed or have a mental health condition.

Chemical imbalances in the brain can trigger mental health conditions or disorders that can be treated with the right medication and therapy, which is good news.

What I absolutely know for sure is that I must continue to see my psychiatrist on a regular basis and take medication every day to keep my mental health in check. If I had continued to do those things after being discharged from the hospital in 2014, I might not have had another bipolar episode in 2019, or maybe it wouldn't have been so severe that I attempted suicide. My refusal to take medication to control my condition or to reach out for help almost cost me my life.

When I was in the middle of my mental health crises in 2014 and 2019, I literally wasn't in my right mind. The person I was then is not the normal caring, compassionate and balanced person I am when I'm taking my medication every day.

3. **Trust those who know you.**
Others will often notice changes in your mental health before you do. Listen to them and let them help you. Since others might notice when I go out of balance before I do, I have asked my husband and sister, who are around me most, to be on the alert for signs I might be spiraling again. I've learned to trust others to help me when I'm in crisis.

4. **Be truthful and open about your condition.**
When I was admitted to the hospital after my second suicide attempt, I never told doctors that I had previously been hospitalized for bipolar. When I was diagnosed with severe depression, I just went along

with it. Doctors can only properly treat you if they have all the facts at their disposal.

5. You will not just "snap out of it."

You can't "just snap out of" clinical depression or a mental health crisis by ignoring it or trying to be more positive. No matter how many people tell you to "just be more positive" or "just get out of the house and go for a walk," you can't if you're severely depressed or in the middle of a mental health crisis. It's like trying to turn on the lights when the electricity isn't working. You need mental health treatment. Do not take matters into your own hands and try to diagnose or treat yourself. Do not self-medicate. Just as you would only trust a doctor to set your broken leg, you should only rely on experts in mental health to treat your mind.

6. A mental health disorder is a condition, just like any other.

If a doctor diagnosed you with high blood pressure and advised you to take medicine and get diet and lifestyle counseling to manage it, you would. You wouldn't question the diagnosis. You wouldn't be ashamed and afraid to share your condition with others. A mental health disorder is a condition, just like high blood pressure or any other. It is nothing to be ashamed of. It needn't define you. It is only one part of you. For example,

"I love sports, I wear glasses, I have high blood pressure, and I am bipolar."

7. The More We Talk about Mental Health, the More Comfortable Others Will Be Hearing and Talking about It.

We have no trouble talking endlessly about our physical health when we get together with family and friends, "I just went to see a new cardiologist. My friend just got diagnosed with cancer, etc." But we don't open up about our mental health. This needs to change or more people will suffer and, even more tragically, die in silence. Now, I have no problem saying that I'm bipolar or mentioning that I have an appointment with my psychiatrist. By being open about it, we help to remove the stigmas and fears surrounding mental health.

8. Forgiveness Is Crucial To Your Recovery.

After my mental health crises, I felt enormous guilt and shame for how I acted during my bipolar episodes. A crucial part of my recovery was realizing that my erratic behavior was due to a mental health condition and that I had to forgive myself for what I had done to myself and others in order to move forward. When my husband Douglas immediately forgave me after my second suicide attempt, it helped me begin to heal. If you are a friend, relative or loved one of someone who has a mental health condition, forgiveness, understanding and compassion will help you heal as well.

9. THERE ARE MILLIONS OF PEOPLE JUST LIKE YOU AND ME.

In the U.S. alone, more than 2.3 million people have been diagnosed with bipolar, and over 50 million Americans (nearly one in five adults) live with a mental health condition, according to the National Institute of Mental Health.

Millions more have undiagnosed mental health issues or can't get the help they need because our health system is geared to treat our bodies instead of our minds. According to *Forbes*, "there are about 28,000 psychiatrists in the U.S. but that number is dwindling rapidly since those practicing are aging. Three in five psychiatrists currently in practice are 55 years of age or older, the AAMC (Association of American Medical Colleges) data shows."

According to the CDC, "Suicide is the 10th leading cause of death in the United States. It was responsible for more than 47,000 deaths in 2019, which is about one death every 11 minutes. The number of people who think about or attempt suicide is even higher. In 2019, 12 million American adults seriously thought about suicide, 3.5 million planned a suicide attempt, and 1.4 million (myself included) attempted suicide. Suicide affects all ages."

10. Get Help

If I can help one person get help in an emergency by reaching out to a family member, neighbor, friend, clergy member, their doctor, psychiatrist, therapist, or calling 911, my story will have made a difference.

If you or someone you know is experiencing emotional distress or thoughts of suicide, help is available. Call NAMI (National Alliance on Mental Illness) at 1-800-950-6264, Monday-Friday, 10 a.m. to 10 p.m. pm., ET. Or *in a crisis text* "NAMI" to 741741 for 24/7, confidential, free crisis counseling. Or call the Suicide Prevention Lifeline 24/7 at 1-800-273-8255. Or call 911.

Acknowledgements

To my husband and soulmate, Douglas Spandau, whose love, support and encouragement saved my life more than once. I'm so grateful that you asked me to be your gym partner. That day, when we did stretching exercises together, has stretched into the most fabulous 40 plus years together.

To my sister Kim, who has always stuck up for me no matter what. I'm glad we "chose" each other. I can never thank you enough for what you've done for Mom. To my brother Mark who loves football even more than I do. To Uncle Eddie and Jeff Lindstrom for being there when my family needed you. To my niece Alicia, and my nephews Chris and Jake, who have brought such joy into my life. Proud doesn't even begin to cover it. To my great nieces Parker and Raegan: remember that Girls Rule The World.

To Linda: we've come a long way from our rubber cone days. Thanks for being the best friend and editor I could have asked for. To you and Chester: Keep dancing!

To Nilsa: I love you Momita!

To Kerry and Patty Reid: I can't thank you enough for changing my life.

To Andrea: thanks for all the fun, especially in Las Vegas!

To my church families at the Unitarian Universalist Congregation of Columbia and Channing Memorial Church.

To Patricia Marshall, Kristen Brack, Kim Harper-Kennedy and everyone at Luminare Press, thank you for making this book a reality.

To all the tireless disability advocates I've had the pleasure of working with including but not limited to: Marni McNeese, Joyce Lehrer, Erica Lewis, Harriet Fisher, Andre Fontaine, Dr. Nollie Wood, Jr., Hal Franklin, Betsy Luecking, Terri Parish, Ginger Palmer and Marian Vessels.

To all the doctors, nurses, and first responders who have cared for me, especially Dr. Stuart Miller, an exceptionally compassionate foot and ankle orthopedist who has treated me since 1997, and my psychiatrist Dr. Angela Onwuanibe along with everyone at Solutions for Mindfulness.

Finally to all the doctors, nurses, hospital workers, medical professionals, caregivers and first responders: you are angels on earth.

CPSIA information can be obtained
at www.ICGtesting.com
Printed in the USA
BVHW042022111221
623802BV00002B/5

9 781643 888293